Letter from the Co-Chairs

Dear Mr. President:

The Department of Justice and the White House Domestic Policy Council first convened the Legal Aid Interagency Roundtable in 2012 because we recognized a simple truth: Federal programs can do a better job for the American people—especially low-income and vulnerable populations—when they include civil legal aid. Armed with this knowledge, the original 18 Federal agencies participating in the roundtable sought new ways to incorporate legal aid into their work. The results of these early initiatives were inspiring, making clear that access to justice helps individuals and families secure basic necessities like health care, housing, employment, and education, while also enhancing family stability and increasing public safety.

You recognized the success of these efforts when you signed a Presidential Memorandum on September 24, 2015 formally establishing the White House Legal Aid Interagency Roundtable (WH-LAIR). U.S. Ambassador to the United Nations Samantha Power announced the Presidential Memorandum on the eve of the adoption of the United Nations' historic 2030 Agenda for Sustainable Development. The Memorandum expands the number of participating agencies, urges these agencies to accelerate and deepen their commitment to legal aid, and directs them to assist the United States in the implementation of Goal 16 of the 2030 Agenda.

This first annual report documents how WH-LAIR has worked over the past four years to inspire innovative interagency collaborations that support and protect individuals who are frequently overlooked and often underserved. It also provides dozens of examples of agencies working together and with legal aid to develop programs that advance their common goals. Finally, the report discusses how the WH-LAIR agencies are collaborating with state and local partners to ensure that the most vulnerable among us receive the fair treatment and equal justice that they deserve.

Although we have made significant advancements in this field, there is still work to be done. We are confident that the White House Legal Aid Interagency Roundtable has laid a foundation that will continue to serve the public well for years to come.

Thank you for your ongoing leadership and for your commitment to one of our country's most fundamental principles: equal justice for all. It is an honor for us to lead this initiative on your behalf and to submit this report to you.

Loretta E. Lynch
Attorney General
United States Department of Justice

Cecilia Muñoz
Director
White House Domestic Policy Council

Message from the Executive Director

It has been an honor to serve as the first Executive Director of the White House Legal Aid Interagency Roundtable (WH-LAIR) and a privilege to work with so many inspiring agency leaders from across the Federal government. Together we have made great progress towards the goal that President Obama set in his Presidential Memorandum, to "increase the availability of meaningful access to justice for individuals and families and thereby improve the outcomes of an array of Federal programs."

Success starts at the top with the leadership of Attorney General Loretta Lynch, White House Domestic Policy Council (DPC) Director Cecilia Muñoz, and their designated co-chairs Principal Deputy Associate Attorney General Bill Baer and Deputy Assistant to the President for Urban Affairs, Justice, and Opportunity in DPC Roy Austin. Credit for LAIR's initial launch and the track record that led to its designation last year as a White House initiative must also be shared with their predecessors former Attorney General Eric Holder, former Special Assistant to the President for Justice and Regulatory Policy in DPC Tonya Robinson, former Associate Attorney General Tony West, and former Principal Deputy Associate Attorney General Stuart Delery.

In the four years since the first LAIR meeting in 2012, our agency representatives—listed in Appendix C—have uncovered important synergies between Federal agency objectives and legal aid. Together with many agency colleagues, they have ensured that our collective policies and priorities translate to meaningful help for the people we all seek to serve. WH-LAIR's success, however, is due not just to its agency members, but also to their active engagement with passionate legal aid advocates throughout the country and essential partners from the judiciary, private bar, charitable foundations, and state, local, and tribal governments. This unprecedented collaboration has produced remarkable results that we are proud to present in this Report

Staffing WH-LAIR with passion and talent were past and present members of the DOJ's Office for Access to Justice: Directors Laurence Tribe, Mark Childress, Deborah Leff, and Lisa Foster; Deputy Director Maha Jweied; Senior Counsels Melanca Clark, Daniel Olmos, Jenni Katzman, Bob Bullock, Andrew Stanner, Helam Gebremariam, Silvia Dominguez-Reese, and Anne Traum; Office Manager Stephan Matthews, and scores of interns hailing from across the country. In addition to her contributions to WH-LAIR's work generally, Senior Counsel Allie Yang-Green deserves special commendation for her exceptional work in production of this Report.

Thanks to the dedication of these individuals and so many other determined Federal colleagues and partners, I am hopeful that the ambitious vision for WH-LAIR will continue to be implemented in the years to come.

Karen A. Lash
WH-LAIR Executive Director

Contents

EXECUTIVE SUMMARY 1

PART I: INTRODUCTION 5

    WHAT IS CIVIL LEGAL AID AND WHY IS IT IMPORTANT TO FEDERAL PRIORITIES? 6

    LAUNCH OF WH-LAIR 10

    HOW WH-LAIR WORKS 13

PART II: LEGAL AID ADVANCING FEDERAL PRIORITIES 19

    ACCESSING HEALTH SERVICES AND IMPROVING HEALTH 20

    EXPANDING ACCESS TO HOUSING AND PREVENTING HOMELESSNESS 22

    STRENGTHENING FAMILIES AND KEEPING CHILDREN IN SCHOOL 24

    KEEPING AMERICANS WORKING 27

    ENHANCING PUBLIC SAFETY AND HELPING CRIME VICTIMS 30

    COMBATTING FRAUD AND PROTECTING CONSUMERS 34

    MEETING THE NEEDS OF SPECIAL POPULATIONS 37

        VETERANS AND SERVICEMEMBERS 37

        TRIBES AND TRIBAL MEMBERS 39

        PEOPLE WITH DISABILITIES 41

        PEOPLE WITH CRIMINAL RECORDS 43

        IMMIGRANTS 44

        DISASTER SURVIVORS 47

PART III: LOOKING AHEAD 49

Appendix A - Presidential Memorandum 53

Appendix B - WH-LAIR's Engagement with Civil Society 57

Appendix C - WH-LAIR Contributors 58

EXECUTIVE SUMMARY

"This Nation was founded in part on the promise of justice for all. Equal access to justice helps individuals and families receive health services, housing, education, and employment; enhances family stability and public safety; and secures the public's faith in the American justice system. Equal access to justice also advances the missions of an array of Federal programs, particularly those designed to lift Americans out of poverty or to keep them securely in the middle class. But gaps in the availability of legal aid—including legal representation, advice, community education, and self-help and technology tools—for America's poor and middle class threaten to undermine the promise of justice for all and constitute a crisis worthy of action by the Federal Government.

~President Barack Obama
Presidential Memorandum Establishing WH-LAIR

Civil legal aid—free legal assistance to low-income and underserved individuals—increases access to justice and alleviates poverty and inequality. With legal aid, a woman may obtain a protection order and escape domestic violence, a homeless veteran may secure stable housing, and a young adult may get their old criminal record expunged and get a job. Though not always appreciated or utilized, legal aid is a critical element of the Federal government's efforts to reduce poverty, protect the most vulnerable among us, and strengthen our communities.

Recognizing the power of legal aid, the White House Legal Aid Interagency Roundtable (WH-LAIR) agencies have been working together since 2012 to integrate legal aid into myriad Federal programs, policies, and initiatives. Co-chaired by the Attorney General and the Director of the White House Domestic Policy Council and staffed by DOJ's Office for Access to Justice, WH-LAIR has engaged Federal grantees, legal aid providers, and Federal agency staff to raise awareness about how legal aid advances Federal priorities. The impressive results include clarifying the scope of dozens of Federal grant programs to include the provision of legal aid that further program goals in the areas of health care, domestic violence, citizenship, homelessness, reentry, and more; developing new training and technical assistance to grantees and legal aid providers; and generating new research about the impact of civil legal aid. WH-LAIR also launched the WH-LAIR website and Toolkit, online resources that provide information about civil legal aid as well as Federal funding opportunities and other resources.

In September 2015, President Obama signed a Presidential Memorandum that formally established the interagency collaboration as a White House initiative. The Memorandum expanded WH-LAIR's mandates to include advancing evidence-based research and data collection of civil legal aid and indigent defense, promulgating best practices, and assisting the United States with implementing Goal 16 of the United Nation's 2030 Agenda for Sustainable Development—which calls on countries to ensure "equal access to justice for all."

EXECUTIVE SUMMARY

This Report is WH-LAIR's first annual report to the President. Part I provides an overview of civil legal aid and WH-LAIR; Part II details WH-LAIR agencies' efforts to improve their programs by incorporating legal aid; and Part III outlines WH-LAIR's plans for the future.

The Report demonstrates that the 22 members of WH-LAIR have taken significant steps to integrate civil legal aid into their programs designed to serve low-income and vulnerable individuals, where doing so can improve their effectiveness and increase access to justice. The strategies that agencies deploy to advance WH-LAIR's mission largely fall into four categories: 1) leveraging resources to strengthen Federal programs by incorporating legal aid; 2) developing policy recommendations that improve access to justice; 3) facilitating strategic partnerships to achieve Federal enforcement and outreach objectives; and 4) advancing evidence-based research, data collection, and analysis. WH-LAIR agencies' efforts in these areas include:

Leveraging resources to strengthen Federal programs by incorporating legal aid
- HHS clarified that legal aid is included in the range of "enabling services" that HHS-funded health centers can provide to meet communities' primary care needs.
- HUD funds fair housing enforcement organizations, including legal aid programs, to assist people who believe they have been victims of housing discrimination.
- Treasury's Internal Revenue Service (IRS) supports legal clinics that provide representation for little to no cost for low-income individuals seeking to resolve disputes with IRS to ensure fairness and integrity in the tax system.
- SSA, ED, and HHS provide legal aid to people with disabilities through the Protection and Advocacy System (P&A) programs and also fund technical assistance to P&A programs providing legal aid.
- CNCS and DOJ fund legal aid lawyers and staff through Elder Justice AmeriCorps to help elder abuse victims and justice AmeriCorps to assist unrepresented immigrant children who have crossed the U.S. border without a parent or legal guardian.
- DOI helps support tribal courts and provides free trainings to tribal judges, prosecutors, and defenders—which include legal aid providers—to strengthen tribal justice systems.

Developing policy recommendations that improve access to justice
- ACUS and DOJ co-chair WH-LAIR's Working Group on Self-Represented Parties in Administrative Hearings, which explores best practices for administrative hearing procedures involving self-represented individuals to increase fairness, accuracy, and efficiency.
- DOL issued the 2016 Workforce Innovation and Opportunity Act final rules, which list legal aid among the services American Job Centers can provide to help youth, adults, and dislocated workers secure employment.
- HHS's Office of Child Support Enforcement outlines opportunities to support self-help strategies for certain legal needs in its proposed rule to modernize the nation's child support program.

- VA issued a directive to advise VA medical facilities on how to refer homeless veterans to legal aid providers for assistance with legal matters, such as child support, outstanding warrants and fines, and to provide office space to legal service providers when possible.
- State, USAID, and DOJ are promoting the creation of the first global network of criminal legal aid providers.

Facilitating strategic partnerships to achieve enforcement and outreach objectives
- FTC developed the Legal Services Collaboration, a nationwide partnership with legal aid, to inform FTC's law enforcement priorities and allow the agency to alert local communities about scams and respond to local concerns.
- CFPB collaborates with legal aid to broaden the reach of the Your Money, Your Goals Toolkit, which helps individuals and families work through short- and long-term financial issues.
- DOJ, DOL, and FTC credit their collaborations with legal aid for enforcement actions ending discriminatory school discipline practices, ensuring language access for injured low-income workers and court users, and helping to shut down illegal practices by car dealers and bogus "work-at-home" scammers.
- EEOC and DOL are working to strengthen their respective collaborative partnerships with civil legal aid providers who can inform the agencies of relevant issues to enhance their enforcement and outreach activities.

Advancing evidence-based research, data collection, and analysis
- DOJ chairs WH-LAIR's Working Group on Access to Justice Indicators and Data Collection, which works to identify national indicators to track the United States' progress in achieving access to justice consistent with Goal 16 of the 2030 Agenda for Sustainable Development.
- NSF sponsored a workshop to advance practitioner-scholar partnerships on access to justice-related research projects, and DOJ, in collaboration with NSF, hosted a Civil Legal Aid Research Workshop to help create a research agenda on Federal priorities at the intersection of civil legal aid, public safety, and criminal justice.
- VA surveys veterans, VA staff, and community participants each year to identify the needs of homeless veterans including their legal needs.
- LSC is undertaking a new national legal needs survey to update the Justice Gap studies of 2005 and 2009.

These are just some of the many WH-LAIR agency actions that expand access to civil legal aid, improve program effectiveness, and enhance the quality of life for families and communities. Although much has been accomplished, there is more work to be done to maximize the performance of Federal programs and ensure meaningful access to justice for all in America.

EXECUTIVE SUMMARY

White House Legal Aid Interagency Roundtable Agencies & Civil Legal Aid Programs in Action

Legal aid helps to create a stable and loving family

"Timmy," a four-year-old boy, had never known a parent other than his 53-year-old grandmother, "Sandra," who cared for him on her own since he was one. On Timmy's behalf, Sandra was receiving Temporary Assistance for Needy Families (TANF) program funds from the Mason County, West Virginia, Department of Health and Human Resources Office. In 2013, she contacted Legal Aid of West Virginia (LAWV) to request help formally adopting her grandson. Through LAWV's WV WORKS Legal Support Project, which receives funds from the state's TANF program, a staff attorney took on the adoption case and helped complete the adoption in 2014. Sandra and Timmy were overjoyed that Timmy's permanent home would be with his loving "ma-ma."

Trafficking victim gains a financial fresh start with legal aid

At risk of homelessness, 18-year-old "Becky" moved in with her boyfriend "Jimmy." Though he initially treated her nicely, Jimmy soon forced her to have sex with other men for money, and work at legal brothels and strip clubs in Nevada and Houston. Eventually Becky escaped, and Jimmy was arrested for his part in a domestic sex trafficking ring. Although finally freed, Becky soon began receiving letters from the IRS for unpaid Federal taxes on nearly $300,000 in the earnings from the legal brothels and strip clubs. Becky turned to Lone Star Legal Aid's Low Income Taxpayer Clinic, a program funded in part with a grant from the IRS, and its lawyer helped Becky document her experience as a trafficking victim who never received any funds. This legal assistance helped eliminate Becky's tax debt and enabled a financial fresh start to help her recover from years of trafficking.

Lawyer's help clears barriers for working mom

Francesca, a 21-year-old single mother of two children, received a job offer to work at a major bank's call center. But when a background check revealed a three-year-old municipal ticket for retail theft, she lost the offer. When she was 18, she got the ticket for taking clothing valued at $20 from a former employer. She knew it was a mistake and vowed not to do it again. She paid the fine thinking that the municipal ticket would not create a criminal record. The recipient of DOL's Face Forward grant referred Francesca to their legal aid partner, Legal Action of Wisconsin, for help. Within a month, a legal aid attorney got Francesca's municipal ticket case reopened and dismissed. After the attorney submitted proof of the dismissal to the state criminal investigation bureau, which cleared Francesca's criminal background report, the bank hired Francesca. After less than eight months on the job, Francesca earned a raise.

Hear Francesca tell her story:
https://blog.dol.gov/2016/11/03/the-ticket-to-new-life/

PART I: INTRODUCTION

"By encouraging Federal departments and agencies to collaborate, share best practices, and consider the impact of legal services on the success of their programs, the Federal Government can enhance access to justice in our communities.

~President Barack Obama
Presidential Memorandum Establishing WH-LAIR

On September 24, 2015, President Barack Obama signed a Presidential Memorandum establishing the White House Legal Aid Interagency Roundtable (WH-LAIR) with a mandate to integrate civil legal aid into a wide array of Federal programs, policies, and initiatives where doing so can improve their effectiveness and enhance justice in our communities. The President noted that, when it comes to increasing access to health services, housing, education, employment, family stability, and public safety for the vulnerable and underserved, civil legal aid can often play a powerful role in meeting these Federal goals and securing the public's trust in the American justice system. But he also recognized that too often legal aid is not available to address these critical priorities.

The Presidential Memorandum directs WH-LAIR to report to the President annually on its progress and to document how it is working to improve the effectiveness and efficiency of Federal activities. This Report highlights the remarkable success WH-LAIR agencies already have achieved.

The Report proceeds in three parts. Part I provides an overview of civil legal aid and how legal aid can advance Federal priorities. Here the Report elaborates on how participating agencies approach and execute WH-LAIR's mission. Part II details how WH-LAIR agencies have incorporated legal aid into a wide range of Federal programs, from accessing health services to meeting the needs of low-income veterans, including concrete examples of how agencies collaborate with legal aid providers to improve their programs and achieve their objectives. Part III outlines the potential future for WH-LAIR, describing how the agencies involved in this effort can continue to work with legal aid partners to achieve their shared goals and strengthen our communities.

PART I: INTRODUCTION

WHAT IS CIVIL LEGAL AID AND WHY IS IT IMPORTANT TO FEDERAL PRIORITIES?

The consequences of limited access to justice reverberate far beyond the courtroom. It hampers our ability to do critical work: to prevent domestic violence and human trafficking; to combat homelessness and predatory lending; to help those in need secure health care and other vital government benefits; to keep kids in school; and to help those with criminal records gain a second chance to succeed.

~Attorney General Loretta E. Lynch
WH-LAIR Co-Chair

> *Most Americans don't realize that you can lose your home, have your children taken away from you, and be a victim of domestic violence in need of a protection order but you have no constitutional right to a lawyer.*
>
> *~James J. Sandman*
> *President, LSC*

What is civil legal aid?

Civil legal aid is free legal assistance to people who have civil legal problems —life-altering problems like foreclosure, eviction, unemployment, debt, and domestic violence. Legal aid also helps people, particularly the most vulnerable among us, access basic necessities such as health care, housing, government benefits, employment, and educational services. Legal aid is especially vital because unlike criminal cases where there is typically a Constitutional right to counsel, there is no right to a lawyer in most civil cases.

Civil legal aid includes direct services by legal aid attorneys and pro bono volunteers who provide representation in court or administrative proceedings or advice to help identify legal issues and develop possible solutions. Legal aid also includes self-help resources and community education delivered through court-based self-help centers, workshops, telephone help lines, online information and chat tools, and downloadable court forms. Legal aid helps Americans of all backgrounds understand their rights and responsibilities and effectively navigate the civil justice system.

Who provides civil legal aid?

Civil legal aid is provided by nonprofit organizations, pro bono volunteers, law schools, and court-based programs.

The largest single funder of civil legal aid for low-income Americans is LSC,[1] which distributes more than 90% of its total Congressional appropriation to 134 independent nonprofit legal aid programs, serving every state and territory with more than 800 offices. LSC is headed by a bipartisan board of directors whose 11 members are appointed by the President and confirmed by the Senate. LSC-funded programs typically help people who live in households with annual incomes at or below 125% of the Federal poverty guidelines.

> The President's Budget for FY 2017 requests $475 million for LSC, the backbone of America's civil legal aid delivery system. Congress appropriated $385 million to LSC for FY 2016, $10 million more than the previous year. Compared to its largest appropriation of $420 million in FY 2010, however, LSC's funding has decreased by 8%, or $35 million. LSC grantees handle the basic civil legal needs of low-income people, addressing matters involving safety, subsistence, and family stability.

LSC-funded organizations comprise only about 25% of the total number of civil legal aid providers nationally. There are hundreds of other nonprofit civil legal aid programs, as well as programs affiliated with law schools and courts, that do not receive LSC funds. Some provide general services while others focus on particular populations or issues (e.g., children, people experiencing homelessness or domestic violence, people with disabilities, or veterans). Some programs coordinate pro bono attorneys or specialize in self-help. Many of these programs do not limit their services based on income, and some serve, for example, older Americans or domestic violence survivors regardless of income. Self-help and informational services are generally available to all.

"Civil legal aid," "legal aid," or "legal services" refers to all of these programs and services. LSC encourages—and all non-LSC programs depend on—leveraging limited resources by partnering with other public and private funders of civil legal aid. Such partners include Federal, state, local, and tribal governments, state-based Interest on Lawyers' Trust Account (IOLTA) programs,[2] access to justice commissions, the private bar, courts, philanthropic foundations, and the business community.

> **Examples of How Legal Aid Expands Its Reach with Pro Bono Volunteers**
>
> ➢ **The American Bar Association Veterans' Claims Assistance Network**, in close coordination with VA, provided unrepresented veterans with pending disability benefits claims the opportunity to work with lawyers to assist them in completing their claims packages for expedited review by VA—at no cost to the veterans.
>
> ➢ **LSC grantees multiply their services by using at least 12.5% of their LSC funds to support pro bono programs.** The volunteers—private attorneys, government attorneys, corporate counsel, law school faculty and students—handled 91,618 cases in 2015 alone, helping over 225,600 people with a wide array of family, housing, employment, and other legal problems.
>
> ➢ **Over 40 Federal agencies participate in the Federal Government Pro Bono Program and promote pro bono work among their attorneys and legal staff.** The program works with legal aid organizations to identify pro bono opportunities that do not pose conflicts for Federal government attorneys, assists attorneys in navigating the rules governing their engagement in pro bono activities, and provides support and resources to volunteers. Attorneys handle family, housing, domestic violence, and consumer law cases, serve as guardians ad litem, draft wills for seniors, provide advice at legal clinics, and teach law to high school students.

Why is civil legal aid important to Federal priorities?

The Federal government advances policy initiatives designed to prevent or end homelessness, domestic violence, hunger, and crime, and Federal agencies support scores of programs that help Americans get an education, a job, and health care. Federal agencies also deploy significant resources to uphold statutory and Constitutional rights that protect veterans and servicemembers, people with disabilities, victims of consumer scams, and many others. These programs should be as effective as possible and have the maximum impact on the greatest number of people.

PART I: INTRODUCTION

Civil legal aid is often an essential element of success. Victims of domestic violence likely need a protection order to keep their abuser away; they may need a child custody or child support order, health insurance, or housing so that they can leave the abuser and provide for their family. Without legal aid, obtaining these critical supports may well be impossible. Eighteen-year-olds with juvenile records may be able to expunge or seal their records, allowing them to obtain a student loan or successfully apply for a job. Without legal assistance to determine their eligibility and help navigate the process, they may not get a second chance in life. And Federal agencies charged with protecting consumers from fraud can more successfully prosecute cases when legal aid lawyers in communities help them identify victims and document their losses. All across the Federal government, many programs will simply work better if they include legal aid. This is also true for the U.S. Government's development work across the globe. International development programs to improve livelihoods, health, and food security are stronger when access to justice is incorporated into their design.

Often, however, government policymakers and social service providers who administer Federal programs are unaware that legal aid can be a critical ingredient to the success of their efforts. WH-LAIR aims to close that knowledge gap and works to leverage legal aid to help Federal agencies better achieve their goals of lifting Americans out of poverty and protecting the most vulnerable among us.

Evidence shows legal aid makes a difference

Although there is still a need for further research on the impact of legal aid, many studies show that people who get legal help achieve better outcomes than people who do not. For example, in housing cases, one study found that 51% of tenants who participated in eviction proceedings without a lawyer lost their homes, while only 21% of tenants with lawyers did.[3] Research on domestic violence suggests that the only service that reduces domestic abuse in the long term is legal assistance.[4] Similarly, a 2014 study indicates that legal interventions, such as expungement of an old criminal record, stems the decline in earnings and may even boost the earnings of individuals reentering society.[5] Studies like these show how legal aid makes a meaningful difference in people's lives and why it should be incorporated into strategies that address a range of Federal priorities.

Studies show investing in legal aid has economic benefits

Ensuring access to legal aid not only prevents financial hardships for those who seek assistance, it can also conserve public dollars by preventing problems like homelessness or health issues that can be extremely costly and harmful to individuals and the public. For example, an HHS-funded medical-legal partnership study concludes, "civil legal aid services can positively impact individual and population health ... [and] ... drive down healthcare costs."[6] Civil legal aid can also help children leave foster care more quickly, improving efficiency and cutting costs in public programs. In Washington State, legal representation for parents in child welfare proceedings resulted in children exiting foster care at a rate that was 11% higher than unrepresented parents and adoptions nearly doubling. This in turn lowers payments to foster parents, subsidies for children's medical care, cash benefits, and the expense of monitoring the foster family.[7] Federal programs that provide for legal aid help achieve these kinds of economic benefits.

The need is great

Currently, available resources for civil legal aid do not meet the need for services. According to the U.S. Census Bureau, in 2015, over 60 million Americans —nearly one in five—qualified for free legal aid from an LSC-funded legal aid program based on their income.[8] Past studies have found that approximately 50% of those seeking legal aid are turned away because of limited resources.[9] These statistics describe only those below or near the poverty line and do not reflect the tens of millions of moderate-income Americans who also cannot afford legal help. According to a recent study, by age 60, nearly four in five Americans will experience some kind of economic hardship, such as relying on a government program for the poor or living at least one year in poverty or very close to it.[10] These Americans cannot afford to hire a private lawyer even when faced with catastrophic events like the potential loss of a home, health care, a job, or educational opportunities. Problems that end up in court can be especially overwhelming for the estimated 75-80% of civil litigants who must represent themselves without the help of a lawyer.[11]

Most people don't know that their problem has a legal solution

The majority of low- and moderate-income Americans do not see the issues they encounter as legal problems.[12] Raising awareness about and increasing the capacity of civil legal aid is critically important to matching people with appropriate services. A family may be concerned about unsafe housing conditions or harassment from debt collectors, but may see these as personal or social problems, or just bad luck, while a legal aid lawyer may be able to identify a legal solution. Research also shows that poor people are twice as likely as their moderate-income counterparts to do nothing to address their civil justice problems, even though they may need the help even more.[13]

Research says:

Going Without a Lawyer

According to reports from state judges:
Arizona: 90% of litigants in domestic violence and probate cases are self-represented
Florida: 80% of divorce cases had at least one litigant without a lawyer
Hawaii: 96% of tenants in landlord-tenant cases and 80% of homeowners in foreclosure cases do not have legal representation
Minnesota: in 71% of family law cases at least one party is self-represented
New York: 99% of New York City tenants in eviction cases were self-represented

Source: Budget Request for Fiscal Year 2017, Legal Servs. Corp.

> *You've also proven that civil legal aid doesn't just open doors to our justice system—it provides a critical reinvestment in the community. Your work saves precious taxpayer dollars by protecting patients' health, increasing access to public benefits, keeping families together, reducing domestic violence, and offering indigent citizens a way out of poverty. And this economic benefit is more important than ever before, as so many of us—at every level of government, and across both the nonprofit and private sectors—have struggled to meet constantly growing demands with increasingly limited budgets.*
>
> ~*Former Attorney General Eric Holder*
> *Keynote Speech, Legal Aid Society of Cleveland Annual Dinner, 2012*

PART I: INTRODUCTION

Launch of WH-LAIR

"Access to legal services matter[s], and it is what can make the difference . . . for [people] with faces and families; in a victim of domestic violence obtaining a restraining order; a homeless veteran getting housing assistance—ten more of whom become homeless in America every day; and a working mom receiving child support. . . .That is why the presidential memorandum . . . that President Obama signed today—which makes permanent an effort to increase access to services for the poor across 20 government agencies—is so important.

~Ambassador Samantha Power
U.S. Permanent Representative to the United Nations

Former Associate Attorney General Tony West and former DPC Special Assistant Tonya Robinson co-chair LAIR meeting on December 6, 2013. (Photo: DOJ)

The White House Domestic Policy Council (DPC) and DOJ convened the Legal Aid Interagency Roundtable (LAIR) in 2012 to improve the outcomes of Federal programs that serve low-income and other vulnerable populations and safeguard their rights by incorporating legal aid. With the support of former Attorney General Eric Holder and DPC Director Cecilia Muñoz, former Associate Attorney General Tony West and DPC Special Assistant Tonya Robinson co-chaired the first LAIR meeting in July 2012, which was attended by representatives from 18 Federal agencies. LAIR was launched and staffed by DOJ's Office for Access to Justice (ATJ), an office that helps spearhead national efforts to improve the civil and criminal justice systems for low-income and underserved populations.

LAIR had three objectives:

1. Identify Federal funding opportunities that could achieve improved outcomes and more efficiently reach program goals by adding civil legal aid partners;
2. Identify opportunities for agency collaborations with legal aid that could improve Federal enforcement and outreach activities; and
3. Identify and eliminate unintended barriers that could prevent legal aid providers from becoming grantees, sub-grantees, or partners in initiatives that serve underrepresented and vulnerable populations.

LAIR's accomplishments included:

➢ Clarification that dozens of grants involving health care, domestic violence, citizenship, homeless veterans, reentry, and more can include legal aid because it furthers program goals;
➢ More than 100 webinars and other presentations to Federal grantees, the civil legal aid community, and Federal agency staff about how legal aid advances Federal priorities;
➢ New training and technical assistance to grantees and legal aid providers;
➢ Research about the impact of civil legal aid; and
➢ Launch of the LAIR website and Toolkit, online resources that provide information about civil legal aid and how it helps advance a broad array of Federal objectives as well as available Federal funding opportunities and other resources.

LAIR also received international recognition as a U.S. national best practice on the Rule of Law on the United Nations' Rule of Law website.

Three years of achievements prompted the President to issue a Presidential Memorandum establishing LAIR as a White House initiative, and it was announced by Ambassador Samantha Power on the eve of the United Nation's Sustainable Development Summit in September 2015. The Presidential Memorandum named the Attorney General and DPC Director as co-chairs and charged White House LAIR (WH-LAIR) with accelerating its activities and expanding its Federal partners.[14] Becoming a White House initiative came with additional mandates to report annually on progress, advance relevant evidence-based research and data collection, and to assist the United States with implementing Goal 16 of the United Nation's 2030 Agenda for Sustainable Development. Goal 16, which calls for the provision of equal access to justice for all, signals the global communities' recognition that access to justice is necessary to end poverty. WH-LAIR's mandate to implement Goal 16 demonstrates to the world that the United States takes the task of improving access to justice seriously.

Presidential Memorandum Establishing the White House Legal Aid Interagency Roundtable

Section 4(a) [WH-LAIR] shall work across executive departments, agencies, and offices to:

(i) improve coordination among Federal programs that help the vulnerable and underserved, so that those programs are more efficient and produce better outcomes by including, where appropriate, legal services among the range of supportive services provided;

(ii) increase the availability of meaningful access to justice for individuals and families, regardless of wealth or status;

(iii) develop policy recommendations that improve access to justice in Federal, State, local, tribal, and international jurisdictions;

(iv) assist the United States with implementation of Goal 16 of the United Nation's 2030 Agenda for Sustainable Development; and

(v) advance relevant evidence-based research, data collection, and analysis of civil legal aid and indigent defense, and promulgate best practices to support the activities detailed in section 4(a)(i)-(iv).

PART I: INTRODUCTION

WH-LAIR and the UN's Sustainable Development Agenda

[W]e commit ourselves to new Sustainable Development Goals, including our goal of ending extreme poverty in our world. We do so understanding how difficult the task may be. We suffer no illusions of the challenges ahead. But we understand this is something that we must commit ourselves to. Because in doing so, we recognize that our most basic bond—our common humanity—compels us to act. ... That's why, today, I am committing the United States to achieving the Sustainable Development Goals.

~President Barack Obama
September 27, 2015
United Nations
Sustainable Development Summit

In September 2015, the United Nations adopted the 2030 Agenda for Sustainable Development—a historic agenda to end extreme poverty while taking action on climate change and inequality, setting forth 17 Goals and 169 associated targets to guide this ambitious task. Among the goals, Goal 16—and specifically target 16.3—recognizes that access to justice is essential to promoting peaceful and inclusive societies for sustainable development. Target 16.3 calls on countries to:

> "Promote the rule of law at the national and international levels and ensure equal access to justice for all."

Unlike past global anti-poverty efforts, which primarily focused on developing countries, the 2030 Agenda applies to every country, no matter its level of development—including the United States. Demonstrating the United States' commitment to the Sustainable Development Goals (SDGs), President Obama charged WH-LAIR to "assist the United States with implementation of Goal 16" in the Presidential Memorandum formally establishing WH-LAIR. The Presidential Memorandum also added to WH-LAIR the Department of State and United States Agency for International Development, both of which offered significant leadership during the United States' participation to develop and adopt the 2030 Agenda.

The 2030 Agenda also calls for the creation of international, regional, and national indicators for all of its goals to help track their progress. In response, WH-LAIR agencies launched the Working Group on Access to Justice Indicators and Data Collection to identify national indicators for Target 16.3.

PART I: INTRODUCTION

How WH-LAIR Works

WH-LAIR deploys a range of strategies to advance its mission. They largely fall into the following four categories:

- Leveraging resources to strengthen Federal programs by incorporating legal aid;
- Developing policy recommendations that improve access to justice;
- Facilitating strategic partnerships to achieve enforcement and outreach objectives; and
- Advancing evidence-based research, data collection, and analysis.

1) Leveraging resources to strengthen Federal programs by incorporating legal aid

To help Federal programs reach their maximum effectiveness and efficiency, as called for in the Presidential Memorandum, WH-LAIR agencies leverage Federal resources by incorporating legal aid into existing funding, training, and technical assistance opportunities to better serve vulnerable and underserved populations.

WH-LAIR member agencies have reviewed numerous Federal grants, recognizing that legal aid for individuals and families living in poverty or near poverty has too often been overlooked, despite the critical contribution it can make to the success of so many programs. As a result, many agencies clarified that dozens of grants can be used by grantees for legal services that further program goals. Examples include DOJ and DOL programs that give people with old criminal records a second chance; VA and DOL grants to help homeless veterans; HHS grants that ensure access to health services and improve prospects for healthy outcomes; and DHS programs to promote immigrant civic integration and prepare permanent residents for citizenship.

USAID, the U.S. Government's lead development agency, works to strengthen access to justice and legal empowerment in partner countries around the world by funding activities that support the provision of legal aid, strategic litigation, access to paralegals, legal clinics, and "know your rights" campaigns and human rights education.

WH-LAIR's interagency activity has also led to agencies working collaboratively to provide funding for legal aid. For example, to advance shared efforts to support successful reentry for people with criminal records, HUD and DOJ together launched the Juvenile Reentry Assistance Program (JRAP) to provide legal aid that reduces or prevents collateral consequences for justice-involved youth living in public housing. Likewise, CNCS and DOJ created "justice AmeriCorps" to increase legal aid to unaccompanied and unrepresented immigrant children and enhance the effectiveness and efficiency of immigration court proceedings.

Another important way to leverage Federal resources is to incorporate legal aid into training and technical assistance (TTA) programs.[15] Whether for the legal aid community to get trained in a new issue impacting Federal priorities or for other service providers to get trained on how legal aid helps address particular problems, TTA can be the critical link to ensuring the success of Federal programs.

> *JRAP is...just one of the many great ideas that have arisen in part from the White House Legal Aid Interagency Roundtable, or WH-LAIR, which brings together 22 Federal agencies in an effort to identify and enhance legal aid opportunities, including for reentering individuals.*
>
> *~Attorney General Loretta Lynch*
> *WH-LAIR Co-Chair*
> *National Reentry Week*
> *Remarks, April 2016*

PART I: INTRODUCTION

> *Legal aid can take many forms, from helping people complete the most basic legal tasks to providing representation in court or at an agency hearing. In many of its forms—both simple and complex—legal aid is an important component of promoting efficiency and fairness in government operations.*
>
> ~Matthew Wiener
> Executive Director, ACUS

For instance, after studying and confirming that medical-legal partnerships (MLPs) improve health outcomes and decrease health costs, HHS began providing TTA about MLPs to community health centers. Similarly, DOJ funds TTA to victim legal assistance network grantees, and a disability advocacy organization was awarded contracts to provide TTA to the SSA-, ED- and HHS-funded Protection and Advocacy legal assistance programs for persons with disabilities.

2) Developing policy recommendations that improve access to justice

In accordance with the Presidential Memorandum's challenge to "develop policy recommendations that improve access to justice," WH-LAIR agencies endeavor to identify opportunities to remove obstacles to legal aid collaborations by issuing policy guidance or new rules. For example, signaling its support for ensuring legal aid to veterans, the VA issued a policy memo to VA hospitals encouraging hospital staff to refer homeless veterans to legal aid providers for assistance with matters such as child support or outstanding warrants or fines, and to provide office space to legal aid providers when possible to facilitate on-site help. Several agencies also published new rules that for the first time include or expand the use of legal assistance to achieve program goals. For example, DOL's 2016 Workforce Innovation and Opportunity Act (WIOA) final rules include legal aid under the list of supportive services for job seekers at American Job Centers, and HHS's Office of Child Support Enforcement outlined opportunities to support self-help strategies for certain legal needs in their proposed rule to modernize the nation's child support program.

WH-LAIR agencies' policy efforts also include developing promising practices. The current centerpiece of this activity involves a Working Group on Self-Represented Parties in Administrative Hearings, launched in 2015 and co-chaired by DOJ's ATJ and ACUS. Federal programs frequently interact with low- and moderate-income people in administrative hearings that affect people's most basic needs—such as establishing, maintaining, or losing eligibility for food assistance, housing subsidies, medical care, and other vital public benefits. Both for agencies and program beneficiaries, it is essential to ensure the fairness and accuracy of these administrative decisions, as well as to increase the efficiency of the procedures when possible. The working group explores best practices for hearing procedures involving the self-represented, drawing on the growing body of case law, studies, and experience in the access to justice field.[16] ACUS is also conducting a research project to develop best practices and make recommendations for Federal agencies to improve fairness and efficiency for the self-represented in administrative hearings.[17] The project was considered by ACUS's Committee on Administration & Management, which approved a draft recommendation. Subject to Council approval, the project will be considered by ACUS's full Assembly at its Plenary Session in December 2016.

3) Facilitating strategic partnerships to achieve enforcement and outreach objectives

To help Federal agencies' enforcement activities and outreach programs more effectively meet their objectives, WH-LAIR agencies partner with legal aid in various ways. As trusted community intermediaries, legal aid providers can give agency staff on-the-ground insights and information from their client work and community engagement. Agencies like FTC, DOJ, and DOL credit their collaborations with legal aid for helping to shut down illegal practices by car dealers and bogus "work-at-home" scammers, ensuring language access for injured low-income workers and court users, and ending discriminatory school discipline practices.

Legal aid providers also help deepen Federal agencies' outreach to low-income and underserved communities. CFPB's collaboration with legal aid broadens the reach of valuable Federal tools like CFPB's Your Money, Your Goals Toolkit, which helps individuals and families work through short- and long-term financial issues. Additionally, HUD, Treasury's IRS, DOL, and SSA collaborated with Pro Bono Net, a national nonprofit organization, to raise awareness about their informational and educational materials to legal aid providers, pro bono volunteers, and self-represented litigants.

4) Advancing evidence-based research, data collection, and analysis

Consistent with the Federal government's commitment to evidence-based policymaking and the Presidential Memorandum's directive to "advance relevant evidence-based research, data collection, and analysis of civil legal aid and indigent defense, and promulgate best practices," WH-LAIR agencies continue to build on early efforts to generate research and evaluate the impact of civil legal aid on their programs and overall mission, including through data collection.

In 2012, NSF sponsored a workshop entitled *Access to Civil Justice: Re-Envisioning and Reinvigorating Research*. The workshop identified key unanswered questions about access to justice that are central to both practice and scholarship, and opened a conversation to advance practitioner-scholar partnerships on specific research projects. The workshop, coupled with NSF's 2013 Dear Colleague Letter: Stimulating Research Related to the Use and Functioning of the Civil Justice System, contributed to numerous and successful joint practitioner-researcher applications to NSF on a range of topics such as studying outcomes from self-help strategies and representation in housing and small claims courts.[18]

Building on these successes, in 2015, DOJ's ATJ and National Institute of Justice (NIJ), in collaboration with NSF, hosted a Civil Legal Aid Research Workshop to help identify a research agenda on Federal priorities at the intersection of civil legal aid, public safety, and criminal justice, including human trafficking, consumer protection, elder abuse, domestic violence, and reentry of formerly incarcerated individuals. The conveners published a report in 2016 summarizing the proceedings and the recommendations of the experts who attended, including their conclusion that the impact of civil legal aid as a tool to empower the lives of low-income people is significantly understudied. A number of key themes emerged, including a request that the Federal government improve data collection on access to justice activity and develop sound Sustainable Development Goal 16 indicators.

> *[W]e have come to value our partnerships with legal aid groups. They have helped us reach out to low-income consumers and those who are economically vulnerable. They play crucial front-line roles to ensure access to justice and promote financial security for consumers who may be unbanked, under-banked, or credit invisible.*
>
> ~Richard Cordray
> Director, CFPB

PART I: INTRODUCTION

This activity and the Presidential Memorandum's directives led to the launch of a WH-LAIR Working Group on Access to Justice Indicators and Data Collection in the summer of 2016, co-led by DOJ's ATJ and Bureau of Justice Statistics. As described on page 12, the 2030 Agenda for Sustainable Development calls for the creation of international, national, and regional indicators for all of its goals.[19] WH-LAIR's narrower charge relates to SDG 16, and the working group is presently focusing on identifying national indicators for target 16.3. The working group received valuable input from a September 2016 Civil Society Consultation on Access to Justice Indicators and Data Collection attended by access to justice experts from across the country.

WH-LAIR and the Open Government Partnership

Launched in 2011 by the United States and seven other countries, the Open Government Partnership (OGP) has grown to a 70-country initiative that aims to secure concrete commitments from governments to promote transparency, empower citizens, fight corruption, and harness new technologies to strengthen governance. In the third U.S. Open Government National Action Plan released in October 2015 and its update released in September 2016, WH-LAIR's activities and collaboration with civil society were included as a national commitment on access to justice.[20]

In keeping with the OGP principles, WH-LAIR has collaborated extensively with civil society both to share its work and learn about the needs of the legal aid community and the people they serve. WH-LAIR has promoted transparency and citizenry empowerment through its active participation in consultations and workshops and through presentations, as well as the publication of the WH-LAIR Toolkit and website.

Working with Civil Society. As documented in Appendix B, WH-LAIR has presented on its goals and activities and how legal aid helps to address national problems like elder abuse and consumer fraud to a number of civil society organizations. WH-LAIR agencies also held listening sessions and gathered information about legal aid's role in disaster response and affordable housing. Additionally, civil society consultations with access to justice experts have served a valuable role in helping WH-LAIR agencies understand their views.

In recognition of WH-LAIR's collaborative efforts, two civil society organizations have bestowed prestigious awards on WH-LAIR: the 2014 National Legal Aid and Defender Association's Justice Through Government Service Award and the 2016 National Center for Medical-Legal Partnership's Medical-Legal Partnership Leadership Award.

Publishing WH-LAIR Toolkit and Website. Originally launched in 2014, the Toolkit was re-issued as the WH-LAIR Toolkit in 2016 with updated content to its three sections:

- Civil Legal Aid 101: an overview of what civil legal aid is and some of the common barriers to accessing civil legal aid
- Case Studies: a series of papers on how legal aid supports a wide range of Federal priorities
- Federal Agency Resources: a listing of more than 100 Federal grants and program activities for which civil legal aid providers are an eligible grantee, sub-grantee, or partner, along with other examples of Federal resources helpful to civil legal aid programs and the people they serve.

The WH-LAIR website also features the Presidential Memorandum, Federal publications of interest to legal aid programs, and periodic blogs about WH-LAIR activities.

PART II: LEGAL AID ADVANCING FEDERAL PRIORITIES

Part II of the Report highlights Federal agencies' work to advance WH-LAIR's mission: to improve the outcomes of Federal programs that serve low-income and other vulnerable populations and safeguard their rights by incorporating civil legal aid. The Report first addresses six Federal priorities related to WH-LAIR's mission:

- Accessing health services and improving health
- Expanding access to housing and preventing homelessness
- Strengthening families and keeping children in school
- Keeping Americans working
- Enhancing public safety and helping crime victims
- Combatting fraud and protecting consumers

The Report then turns to agencies' efforts to partner with legal aid organizations to meet the needs of special populations:

- Veterans and servicemembers
- Tribes and tribal members
- People with disabilities
- People with criminal records
- Immigrants
- Disaster survivors

The Federal activities highlighted in Part II represent both the activities that were inspired by or directly resulted from the agencies' participation in WH-LAIR, and those that began prior to the launch of WH-LAIR but are aligned with WH-LAIR's mission. By capturing the most notable of all those activities, this Report seeks to be a comprehensive resource for Federal agencies and the public to learn about how WH-LAIR agencies are using legal aid to improve their programs and better serve low-income and vulnerable people.

PART II: LEGAL AID ADVANCING
FEDERAL PRIORITIES

ACCESSING HEALTH SERVICES AND IMPROVING HEALTH

> *Civil legal aid ensures that more Americans have access to good nutrition, safe housing and other basic human necessities that are essential to overall health and well-being. It also plays a key role in HHS' efforts to provide our most vulnerable citizens with access to quality, affordable health care services.*
>
> ~Sylvia Mathews Burwell
> Secretary, HHS

Many vulnerable and low-income individuals face serious obstacles to accessing health services and improving health. These include high costs, no insurance, cultural and linguistic barriers, and the lack of community-based preventative services, primary care, and treatment for mental health conditions and substance use disorders. The lack of access to preventive services and treatments often leads to an increase in avoidable long-term medical expenditures and a decrease in overall health. This also harms society at large by lowering productivity and placing an increased burden on the health care system.

People of color and low-income individuals are among those most likely to be uninsured and less likely to receive necessary health care.[21] Uninsured individuals are more likely to delay or forgo necessary health services, which can lead to more serious conditions and can result in hospitalizations from preventable health problems.

HHS and other Federal agencies increasingly recognize the impact of social conditions on health outcomes and legal aid's role in addressing these conditions. These agencies now encourage legal aid providers to collaborate with health care teams to detect, address, and prevent health-harming social conditions that have their roots in legal problems. Legal aid can help secure health care coverage or health benefits by appealing erroneous administrative denials of benefits or insurance. Through legal clinics in medical facilities and medical-legal partnerships (MLPs), legal aid can improve patient health by, for example, addressing substandard housing conditions such as mold, rodent, or insect infestations that increase use of costly emergency room visits for asthma attacks.[22] Legal aid also helps prepare legal documents to ensure patients' wishes are met, such as living wills and powers of attorney for medical care and financial affairs.[23]

WH-LAIR promotes evidence-backed innovations such as MLPs and supports Federal agencies' efforts to incorporate legal aid to help vulnerable and low-income people access health services and improve health.

 Research says:

HHS-funded pilot medical-legal partnership study concludes:

"...civil legal aid services can positively impact individual and population health," including "significant reduction in stress and improvement in health and wellbeing after receiving [legal] services" such as for housing, public and disability benefits, employment, and debt collection problems. Researchers also found integrating legal services into the healthcare setting "drives down healthcare costs."

Source: Daniel Atkins, Shannon Mace Heller, Elena DeBartolo & Megan Sandel, Medical-Legal Partnerships and Healthy Start: Integrating Civil Legal Aid Services into Public Health Advocacy, 35 J. Legal Med. 195, 196, 205, 207 (2014).

Examples of WH-LAIR agencies' efforts in this area include:

➢ **HHS clarifies that community health centers can provide health-related legal aid.** In recognition of the link between health and legal needs for vulnerable and low-income populations, in 2014, HHS's Health Resources and Services Administration (HRSA) clarified that legal aid may be included in the range of "enabling services" that HRSA-funded health centers can provide to meet the primary care needs of the population and communities they serve. Subsequently, the FY 2015 Expanded Services Supplement Funding opportunity allowed health centers to propose enabling services that could be supported with the funding, which could include access to legal services for patients.

PART II: LEGAL AID ADVANCING FEDERAL PRIORITIES

- **HHS provides training and technical assistance to community health centers (CHCs) and legal aid to develop and strengthen MLPs.** HHS's HRSA awarded a national cooperative agreement to the National Center for Medical-Legal Partnership (NCMLP) to support the growth of quality MLPs in CHCs. NCMLP provides webinars and other training as well as consults with CHCs' staff to build awareness of patients' legal needs and the MLP model and to strengthen the capacity of those CHCs that were early adopters of the MLP. NCMLP has provided specialized assistance to dozens of CHCs and reached many more through webinars and issue papers.

- **VA establishes MLP Taskforce to increase access to legal aid in VA healthcare facilities.** In 2016, VA created a department-wide MLP Taskforce to guide and encourage the growth of MLPs throughout VA healthcare facilities. Currently with at least 12 MLPs in six different states, the VA MLP Taskforce offers regular training sessions for potential new MLP sites, and is developing a VA-specific MLP toolkit for VA clinicians and staff.

- **HHS clarifies that Ryan White HIV/AIDS Program services can include legal aid.** The policy guidance from HHS's HRSA regarding allowable uses of funds includes legal services to or on behalf of the individual living with HIV/AIDS for legal matters related to or arising from their disease, such as assistance with public benefits and preparation of living wills.

- **HHS's healthcare outreach programs include legal aid programs among their grantees.** HHS's Centers for Medicare & Medicaid Services (CMS) funds the Connecting Kids to Coverage program that supports efforts to reach out to families with children eligible for Medicaid and the Children's Health Insurance Program, and helps get them covered. The 2016 grant awardees included several legal aid programs. Additionally, the Navigator program supports in-person assistance for consumers who are shopping for and enrolling in coverage through a Health Insurance Marketplace. The 2016 grant awardees include legal aid programs.

- **HHS is developing a model fair hearing request form for Medicaid program participants.** Participants have the right to a hearing when the Medicaid agency has taken an adverse action against an individual, but may not know how to ask for a hearing. HHS's CMS is developing a model Medicaid fair hearing request form that can be used by states and other stakeholders.

- **LSC funds a Healthy Justice Partnership Project in New Orleans to launch an MLP and increase pro bono legal services.** In 2015, LSC awarded a pro bono grant to Southeast Louisiana Legal Services and its partner organizations to launch an MLP integrating legal aid and healthcare in eight community-based health clinics. The MLP will increase access to legal aid through new and expanded pro bono services delivered by volunteer lawyers, paralegals, and law students; provide services on critical disability, Medicaid, and housing issues; and seek to measure improved health and legal outcomes under the project.

Careworker gets needed benefits through legal aid

For 35 years, "Maxine" guided nursing home patients through their daily routines of getting up, getting dressed, eating and bathing. Being a Nurse's Aide was the only job she knew, but after coming down with a serious illness and breaking her hand, Maxine could no longer work. With no income, Maxine lost her home. After getting denied Social Security disability benefits, Maxine spent two years sleeping in shelters, friends' homes, or her car. With no home and no way to work, her doctor at the HHS-funded Council Bluffs Community Health Center referred her to a medical-legal partnership attorney at LSC-funded Iowa Legal Aid. The attorney worked with Maxine's doctor to properly document Maxine's many medical issues, successfully appealing to the Social Security Administration. With more than $800 a month in disability benefits, as well as a lump sum for back benefits, Maxine moved into a new home. Iowa Legal Aid's work also enabled her to obtain retroactive coverage of Medicaid, which allowed Medicaid to cover care delivered by the Council Bluffs Community Health Center that was previously uncompensated.

PART II: LEGAL AID ADVANCING FEDERAL PRIORITIES

> *Legal aid is an essential tool that paves the way for many Americans to find a safe and decent place to call home.*
>
> ~Julián Castro
> Secretary, HUD

Legal aid supports Federal civil rights enforcement for residents

In 2015, Texas RioGrande Legal Aid and the University of Texas Environmental Law Clinic filed a complaint with the Department of Transportation's Civil Rights Office alleging race discrimination in violation of Title VI of the Civil Rights Act of 1964 relating to a proposed new highway that would have, among other things, displaced hundreds of households and businesses in a historic African-American community and destroyed or isolated homes from the community's schools, churches, hospitals, and local businesses. In DOJ's role coordinating Title VI enforcement across the Federal government, DOJ worked closely with the Department of Transportation, including by facilitating communications with legal aid, other housing advocates, HUD, and the relevant state agencies, leading to a settlement agreement that included monetary and nonmonetary compensation for homeowners and renters, as well as local businesses and churches.

EXPANDING ACCESS TO HOUSING AND PREVENTING HOMELESSNESS

On any given night, more than a half-million people in the United States are homeless — sleeping outside, in an emergency shelter or a transitional housing program.[24] Among them, about 36 percent are families with children.[25]

While some experience homelessness, others struggle to hold on to their homes. The situation has been exacerbated by the recent recession and foreclosure crisis. Foreclosure-rescue and mortgage-modification scammers prey on struggling homeowners by making promises they cannot keep, such as guaranteeing to "save" a home or lower the mortgage, usually for a fee. And many low-income tenants face evictions or substandard living conditions.

To address these obstacles to stable housing, many Federal programs provide services to Americans in need, including legal aid that effectively addresses barriers to housing and advances program goals. For example, legal aid can help by preventing unlawful evictions of tenants in government-subsidized housing, private housing, or foreclosure properties, assisting with utility-related issues, and by stopping landlords from taking advantage of post-disaster conditions. Legal aid also educates, advises, and represents families in foreclosure proceedings, and helps remove obstacles to permanent housing by removing or mitigating old criminal records and correcting credit histories.[26]

WH-LAIR assists Federal agencies' efforts to address homelessness and increase access to housing for the vulnerable and underserved by identifying opportunities to include legal aid in housing-related services and to partner with legal aid to support government enforcement activities.

Examples of WH-LAIR agencies' efforts in this area include:

➢ **HUD's Community Development Block Grant (CDBG) program allows using funds for legal aid necessary to access affordable housing.** The CDBG program provides communities with resources to address a wide range of community development needs. It funds services to ensure decent affordable housing, provides public services to the most vulnerable in our communities, and creates jobs through the expansion and retention of businesses. Legal services are an allowable use of CDBG funds.[27]

➢ **HUD's Emergency Solutions Grants (ESG) program allows using funds for legal aid necessary to regain housing stability.** The ESG program provides grants to states and local government to carry out various activities to assist families and individuals who are homeless or at risk of homelessness. The eligible activities include legal services for homeless families and individuals in emergency shelters (if other appropriate legal services are unavailable or inaccessible) and legal services necessary to help eligible families and individuals obtain permanent housing or regain stability in that housing.

PART II: LEGAL AID ADVANCING
FEDERAL PRIORITIES

- **VA's Supportive Services for Veteran Families (SSVF) Program includes legal aid among the supportive services provided to veterans and their families with housing needs.** In an effort to improve very low-income veteran families' housing stability, SSVF grantees provide eligible families with outreach, case management, and assistance in obtaining VA and other benefits. In 2015, over 30% of SSVF grantees provided legal aid to the veteran families they serve.[28]

- **CNCS and HUD fund the VISTA Affordable Housing Preservation Project (VAHPP) to preserve, maintain, and improve Federally subsidized housing through legal aid and other services.** In 2016-2017, 45 VISTA (Volunteers In Service To America) members in this program will serve more than 18,000 low-income families living in Federally subsidized housing in at least 15 cities through legal support and community organizing. To raise awareness about VISTA and legal aid generally, CNCS and DOJ published the Guide to the AmeriCorps VISTA Program for Legal Services Organizations.

- **HUD's Fair Housing Initiatives Program (FHIP) supports legal aid to enforce fair housing laws.** FHIP provides funding to fair housing enforcement organizations to assist people who believe they have been victims of housing discrimination. FHIP organizations, including legal aid programs, partner with HUD to provide legal assistance and refer people to other HUD-certified state or local government agencies that handle complaints of housing discrimination.

- **DOJ collaborates with legal aid providers to enforce the Fair Housing Act by bringing actions to redress discriminatory housing practices.** Many enforcement actions by DOJ's Civil Rights Division involve practices that threaten the housing rights of very low-income persons who, without access to housing, are in danger of being homeless. These include cases on behalf of low-income women who face sexual harassment by their landlords or by the official who administers their housing subsidies; enforcement actions against local governments that try to exclude group homes and transitional housing for people with disabilities who are at risk of becoming homeless or being institutionalized; and investigations and enforcement actions involving exclusionary zoning practices that restrict the development of and access to affordable or low-income housing for families.

- **HUD's Jobs Plus program addresses entrenched poverty among public housing residents through a number of supportive services, including legal aid.** The Jobs Plus program offers targeted housing developments with various incentives and supports including employer linkages, job placement and counseling, educational advancement, and financial counseling. The types of legal aid services that may be provided with grant funds include helping people with expunging old criminal records.

- **HUD is developing guidance for Public Housing Authorities (PHAs) that will identify best practices related to subsidized lease grievances and hearings.** HUD recognizes that there may be differences among PHAs in how they conduct lease termination proceedings, many of which involve tenants without legal assistance, and wants to ensure compliance with HUD's regulations, increase uniformity among PHAs, and share best practices.

 Research says:

2/3 of low-income tenants receiving full legal representation in eviction cases stayed in their homes as compared to 1/3 of unrepresented tenants. Represented tenants also received almost five times the financial benefit, such as damages or cancellation of past due rent, as those without full representation.

Source: Boston Bar Association Task Force on the Civil Right to Counsel, The Importance of Representation in Eviction Cases and Homelessness Prevention 2 (2012)

PART II: LEGAL AID ADVANCING
FEDERAL PRIORITIES

> *Legal aid lawyers play a unique and critical role in protecting the rights of children and families, and access to legal services can make the difference in preventing homelessness, helping families stay together, and helping parents get jobs to support their families.*
>
> ~Mark Greenberg
> Acting Assistant Secretary
> HHS Administration for
> Children and Families

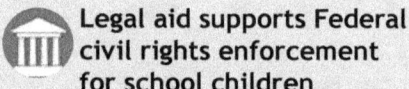

Legal aid supports Federal civil rights enforcement for school children

DOJ's Civil Rights Division received significant assistance from the Legal Aid Society of Palm Beach County with an investigation of the School District of Palm Beach County, Florida, into complaints that the District failed to enroll children based on their or their parents' national origin or immigration status, and that its system of discipline discriminated against students based on national origin and limited English proficiency. The investigation resulted in a pathbreaking settlement between the District and DOJ to prevent and address discrimination in school enrollment, student discipline, and policing.

STRENGTHENING FAMILIES AND KEEPING CHILDREN IN SCHOOL

Today, poverty continues to strain family stability and impede the education of our children. The difficult challenges of substance use disorders, mental health conditions, and domestic violence, often occurring together, bring additional stresses to families that may lead to government removal of children from their parents and placement in the child welfare system, a system that struggles with racial disproportionality and has been found to achieve poor outcomes for children and families.

At the same time, America's prison population has grown dramatically over several decades, increasing the number of children with incarcerated parents, and 2.7 million children in the United States now have at least one parent in prison.[29] Likewise, our public schools continue to face challenges in providing a safe, inclusive, and positive school environment for our most vulnerable, and often impoverished, students. In the 2013-2014 school year, black boys were subjected to suspensions and expulsions at a rate three times higher than that of the overall student body.[30] Moreover, two-thirds of students who faced disciplinary physical restraint or seclusion were students with disabilities.[31]

Federal agencies work on multiple fronts to address the needs of vulnerable and low-income families and children. They administer public benefits programs, oversee the child support enforcement program, fund services for youth involved in the criminal justice system, provide funding and technical assistance to improve the quality of legal representation for parents and children in child welfare proceedings, and provide support to state and local educational programs. Many of these programs partner with legal aid to improve their program outcomes.

Legal aid assists families that need access to public benefits by helping to determine eligibility, complete applications, and appeal erroneous denials or reductions. When child support is at issue, legal aid helps enforce or modify child support orders to secure payments or adjust the amounts when necessary. In addition, to keep children in school, legal aid can explain education laws and school discipline policies to families and propose alternatives to potentially harmful policies of expulsion, lengthy time away from school, and referral to the criminal justice system for non-violent behavioral issues. Legal aid can also advise and represent parents of children with special needs to ensure schools provide them with services. Homeless and foster youth can remain in their schools of origin with the help of legal aid when their living situations change. Legal aid can also remove barriers to learning by addressing immigration, consumer fraud, debt, housing, health, and domestic violence issues.[32]

WH-LAIR supports Federal agencies' efforts to partner with legal aid in their programs to strengthen family stability and support education by helping families to access public benefits, child support, and other critical services.

Examples of WH-LAIR agencies' efforts in this area include:

- ➤ **HHS's Office of Child Support Enforcement (OCSE) includes legal aid and self-help resources to improve child support compliance.** OCSE, an office within HHS's Administration for Children and Families (ACF), promotes responsible parenting and family self-sufficiency by working to ensure that both custodial and non-custodial parents are able to provide for their children. OCSE now expressly allows states to include legal aid in programs that provide an alternative to civil contempt for nonpayment of child support in order to improve compliance and regular payments, thereby increasing parents' trust and confidence in the child support process. OCSE also issued a memorandum in 2013 for its Parenting Time Opportunities to Children program clarifying that partnering with legal aid is a permissible activity within the program. OCSE plans to provide extensive training and technical assistance to state child support agencies, including opportunities to support self-help for certain legal needs, following the publication of their final rule to modernize the nation's child support program and increase its flexibility and efficiency in securing reliable support for families.

- ➤ **HHS clarifies its program language to allow legal aid as part of their services to vulnerable children and families.** For FY 2016, HHS's ACF added clarifying language allowing legal aid as a component of a collaborative practice or strategy to address issues facing children and families experiencing domestic violence, address human trafficking within the child welfare population, and support implementation of the Indian Child Welfare Act.

- ➤ **HHS is working to improve the quality of legal representation for children and parents in child welfare proceedings.** The Court Improvement Program, administered by the Children's Bureau, within the Administration for Children Youth and Families (ACYF) of HHS's ACF, is working to improve the quality of legal representation for children and parents in child welfare proceedings across the country by supporting research, training, and data analysis efforts, and providing technical assistance to judges and attorneys. ACYF is developing guidance strongly encouraging all state and local child welfare agencies and Court Improvement Programs to work together to ensure that all parties in child welfare proceedings receive high-quality legal representation at all stages of a case.

- ➤ **ED's program to improve the educational and developmental outcomes of children in distressed communities allows using program funds for legal aid among other services.** ED's Promise Neighborhoods Program works to create a continuum of services that improve the educational and developmental outcomes of children and youth in our most distressed communities through a variety of services including legal aid.

 Research says:

In cases where a barrier to education was an issue for low-income children—such as suspension or expulsion, lack of appropriate supports for children with special needs, lack of language accommodation, and refusal to enroll, especially for homeless children—LSC-funded Legal Aid Society of Cleveland was successful in removing that barrier in 85% of those cases, helping to ensure that children stay in school and on a path to a better life.

Source: Legal Aid Soc'y of Cleveland, 2015 Annual Report 3 (2016).

PART II: LEGAL AID ADVANCING
FEDERAL PRIORITIES

> **Father and daughter get parenting support from legal aid**
>
> "Daron" was a dedicated father to his young daughter, for whom he regularly paid child support. When his work schedule was reduced and his earnings dropped, he sought help from the Alameda County Superior Court Family Law Facilitator's office, which is funded in part by HHS/ACF's Child Support Enforcement Program. A staff attorney there helped him request a modified child support order that would reflect his pay cut. The lawyer then explained how Daron could also request increased visitation time with his daughter and take on more parenting responsibility. Staff from the court Family Law Facilitator's Office attended the hearing to provide legal information and procedural guidance to Daron. The court made the proposed changes and Daron's payments were reduced to an amount that he could afford. He also began picking his daughter up from school and eating dinner with her twice a week, before returning her to her mother.

➢ **DOJ's Office of Juvenile Justice and Delinquency Prevention (OJJDP) oversees programs that include legal aid to support young fathers and justice-involved youth.** OJJDP administers the Second Chance Act Strengthening Relationships Between Young Fathers and Their Children: A Reentry Mentoring Project, which helps young fathers transition from secure confinement facilities back to their families by providing mentoring and employment assistance, including legal aid.

➢ **HHS, ED, and SSA fund Protection and Advocacy (P&A) System programs that provide advocacy services to children and adults with disabilities.** P&A programs are independent state-based programs that provide legal representation and other advocacy services to persons with disabilities, including individuals with developmental disabilities, mental illness, and other impairments, such as visual or hearing impairments.

➢ **USDA releases a Supplemental Nutrition Assistance Program (SNAP) guidance package to share best practices with states.** USDA developed guidance on informing SNAP (formerly known as food stamps) clients about their rights, including the right to a fair hearing, in all written correspondence. These practices by USDA's Food and Nutrition Service in 2015 were designed to help SNAP participants and applicants, including families and their children, as well as state agencies administering the program, better understand their responsibilities.

KEEPING AMERICANS WORKING

Every American who wants a job should be able to work, and those who lose their jobs should be assisted in getting back to work. While our economy is growing, too many Americans still face challenges securing employment or addressing job-related issues while employed. In particular, those re-entering the workforce after incarceration face significant barriers to employment. Many people with steady employment also face hardships. Some employers misclassify workers and call them independent contractors instead of employees, depriving them of critical protections including family and medical leave, overtime, minimum wage, and unemployment insurance. Additionally, many people—looking for employment or already on the job—find themselves victims of illegal discrimination based on race, color, sex, national origin, religion, age, sexual orientation, gender identity, disability, or genetic information.

Recognizing the importance of employment in lifting Americans out of poverty, DOL and other Federal agencies fund various programs to help American workers and the unemployed, and many of them partner with legal aid. Legal aid helps workers secure the wages and benefits they are entitled to by representing employees at administrative hearings and helps ensure safety in the workplace. Legal aid also assists those with criminal records by helping to expunge or seal old records, reinstate a revoked or suspended driver's license, untangle outstanding court debt issues, modify child support orders, and secure certificates of rehabilitation, dramatically increasing their ability to obtain and keep a job. In addition, job seekers or employees who are discriminated against in the workplace can turn to legal aid for help.[33]

WH-LAIR works with EEOC, DOL, and other Federal agencies to incorporate legal aid into their programs to improve outcomes by helping remove barriers to employment and protecting workers from an unsafe work environment, denial of benefits, and fraud.

Examples of WH-LAIR agencies' efforts in this area include:

➢ **DOL's new Workforce Innovation and Opportunity Act's final rules for American Job Centers include legal aid among services that can be offered to help job seekers.** Rules published in 2016 to implement the Workforce Innovation and Opportunities Act list legal aid among the services American Job Centers—also known as One Stop Career Centers—can provide to help youth, adults, and dislocated workers secure employment.

➢ **HHS makes clear that states can use Temporary Assistance for Needy Families (TANF) funds for employment-related legal assistance.** The TANF program, administered by HHS's Administration for Children and Families, Office of Family Assistance, provides funds to states to help needy families achieve self-sufficiency and provide support for job preparation and employment in addition to other services. HHS has clarified that states may use TANF funds to help resolve legal problems that are a threat to family stability or undermine the employment of needy parents and youth.[34]

> *Legal aid is essential to closing persistent opportunity gaps and to creating shared prosperity in an economy that works for everyone.*
>
> ~Thomas Perez
> Secretary, DOL

 Research says:

Evidence suggests that legal interventions such as expungement and reducing a felony to a misdemeanor stem the decline in earnings and may even boost earnings for people returning from a period of incarceration. Halting the decline in earnings suggests that the interventions make a meaningful difference in people's lives and are key components of an effective employment reentry strategy.

Source: Jeffrey Selbin & Justin McCrary, Got Clean Slate? New Study Suggests that Criminal Record Clearing May Increase Earnings (2014)

PART II: LEGAL AID ADVANCING
FEDERAL PRIORITIES

Legal aid supports Federal civil rights enforcement for workers

DOL and DOJ opened a joint investigation when the Northwest Justice Project, an LSC-funded legal aid program, filed a national origin discrimination complaint alleging that the state of Washington's Department of Labor and Industries failed to give meaningful access to limited English proficiency workers who speak Bosnian, Cambodian (Khmer), and Spanish to the state's workers compensation program. The legal aid organization's ongoing support helped lead to a memorandum of agreement outlining the state agency's dedication to implementing a new language access program, ensuring limited English proficient individuals have full access to its programs, activities, and information.

➢ **VA's Supportive Services for Veteran Families (SSVF) program allows using program funds for legal aid for issues that affect a veteran's employability.** The SSVF program promotes housing stability among very low-income veteran families residing in or transitioning to permanent housing and provides a range of supportive services, including legal aid, to eligible veteran families. Recognizing that multiple legal needs are among the highest unmet needs for very low-income and homeless veterans, VA encourages SSVF program grantees to provide, or assist participants in obtaining, legal aid in order to help remove obstacles to employment when it can help with permanent housing.

➢ **DOL's program for ensuring workplace safety includes legal aid trainers.** Legal aid programs are among the awardees of DOL's Susan Harwood Training Grant to train and educate workers and employers about ensuring safety in the workplace. This program provides training and education for workers and employers on the recognition, avoidance, and prevention of safety and health hazards in their workplaces, and the obligation to inform workers of their rights and employers of their responsibilities under the Occupational Safety and Health Act. Target audiences include underserved and low-literacy employees and workers in high-hazard industries.

➢ **EEOC collaborates with legal aid to provide training and to learn about employment discrimination-related issues in communities.** EEOC's field offices are working to strengthen their partnership with local legal aid offices to conduct outreach for employers and employees, train legal aid staff about the laws enforced by the EEOC, and identify employment discrimination-related issues, problems, or concerns that legal aid staff encounter in their communities.

➢ **DOJ and DOL expand legal aid to address collateral consequences for people with criminal records.** Several large grant programs—such as the DOJ Second Chance Act (SCA) grants and DOL Reentry Employment Opportunities (REO) grants—now allow for the use of Federal funds to pay for legal assistance to secure driver's licenses, expunge old criminal records, modify child support orders, and litigate inappropriate denials of housing or employment and violations of the Fair Credit Reporting Act for people returning to their communities from a period of incarceration.

➢ **DOL develops a "Know Your Rights" video series in English and Spanish covering topics common to legal aid clients.** DOL's Wage and Hour Division developed the "Know Your Rights" video series in English and Spanish to provide workers with useful basic information in different scenarios that workers encounter in the workplace. DOL's Occupational Safety & Health Administration also produced the "Workers' Safety and Health Rights on the Job" video that legal aid or other service providers can show in waiting rooms or other similar areas.

PART II: LEGAL AID ADVANCING
FEDERAL PRIORITIES

- **DOL issues guidance on the state-administered Unemployment Insurance (UI) program to ensure access to unemployment benefits regardless of one's disability, language limitations, age, or race.** DOL is actively promoting improved state processes for the UI program pursuant to the guidance. DOL also has instituted new accountability processes that include a new mandatory self-assessment tool for states to ensure they have necessary operational processes for customer access to UI program services.

- **DOJ trains legal aid providers on legal protections for immigrant workers.** In 2016, DOJ's Civil Rights Division has conducted in-person presentations to several legal aid organizations nationwide on employment discrimination based on citizenship, immigration status, and national origin. These presentations provide legal aid staff with information about worker protections under the statutes that DOJ enforces and how to file complaints, as well as free resources that are available to legal aid organizations.

- **LSC funds a "Lawyers for Entrepreneurs Project" to help low-income entrepreneurs starting or expanding community businesses.** In 2015, LSC awarded a pro bono grant to Legal Services of Eastern Missouri to leverage the resources and skills of attorneys to provide free legal assistance and education to low-income entrepreneurs starting or expanding community businesses, with an emphasis on minority and women entrepreneurs who have limited access to capital.

Lawyer steers Ruben through obstacles to steady finances, family and job

After release from jail and completion of a 90-day substance abuse treatment program, "Ruben" sought help from Bay Area Legal Aid, Contra Costa, CA. Ruben's attorney helped him stabilize several key areas of his life, including advising him on driver's license reinstatement, his Section 8 housing status, family law matters and consumer/credit issues. These services helped him reunite with his family, secure employment, and be evaluated "low risk" on the Probation Department's assessment tool. Bay Area Legal Aid's reentry work is supported by HHS's Community Centered Responsible Fatherhood Ex-Prisoner Reentry Pilot Project, and DOJ's Second Chance Act Adult Reentry Program for Planning and Demonstration Project.

PART II: LEGAL AID ADVANCING FEDERAL PRIORITIES

ENHANCING PUBLIC SAFETY AND HELPING CRIME VICTIMS

Millions of people in the United States are victims of crime. More than one in three women in the United States has been the victim of domestic violence;[35] approximately 10% of people age 60 and older and close to 50% of people with dementia are victims of elder abuse;[36] and over 20 million people around the world, including in the United States, are subjected to forced labor and sex trafficking.[37] Low-income communities, particularly communities of color, are among those that experience the highest crime rates in our country.[38] These communities feel the impact of crime acutely while also experiencing a criminal justice system that often fails to provide indigent defendants with the legal assistance they are entitled to. Crime victims also encounter challenges navigating the justice process, which can impact their sense of fairness, satisfaction, and safety. Many receive little to no assistance understanding and asserting their rights, including to be heard and to participate. To ensure public safety, crime victims and their families need help to regain a sense of normalcy in their lives; communities need to take action to prevent and deter crime; and indigent defendants need competent counsel and access to appropriate services to ensure the fair administration of justice and reduce recidivism.

Many WH-LAIR agencies have developed programs to address the staggering number of crime victims, including victims of domestic violence, elder abuse, and human trafficking. Because legal aid is critical to meet victims' short- and long-term needs and can help keep communities safe, many relevant Federal programs include legal aid. Legal aid helps victims of crime with a range of services to stabilize their lives, including by helping them secure housing, medical assistance, public benefits, immigration relief, education, employment, and child custody orders. Additionally, legal aid helps secure visas for immigrant victims of crime like domestic violence and human trafficking and identifies recurring problems that can lead to involvement in the criminal justice system. Legal aid also prevents future incidents of violence by obtaining, renewing, and enforcing protective orders for clients, providing resources to law enforcement and holding perpetrators accountable.[39]

Some WH-LAIR agencies also help law enforcement prevent crime and keep our communities safe while at the same time ensuring that our criminal justice system treats defendants fairly by providing effective assistance of counsel. This is particularly important given the collateral consequences of being involved in the criminal justice system and the subsequent civil justice problems that can often arise.

WH-LAIR supports Federal agencies incorporating legal aid into their victim services and crime prevention programs and similar efforts supporting indigent defense to strengthen the criminal justice system, both of which are important tools to promote the stability necessary to preventing future crime.

> *Public safety depends on public trust. Legal aid helps rebuild faith and confidence in the justice system by helping crime victims rebuild their lives, by giving people with criminal records a second chance in life, and by working as trusted community partners with law enforcement.*
>
> ~Lisa Foster, Director
> DOJ Office for Access to Justice

Meeting the legal needs of crime victims

DOJ's Office for Victims of Crime recently published a final rule for the Victims of Crime Act program that coincided with substantial increases in victim assistance funding. Congress raised the Crime Victims Fund spending level from $745 million in FY 2014 to more than $2.3 billion in FY 2015, and to more than $3 billion in FY 2016. Consistent with the 2013 Vision 21 Transforming Victim Services Report's discussion of unmet legal needs, efforts to raise awareness about using victim assistance funds for legal aid has resulted in increased resources to meet those needs. For example, in 2016, California awarded more than $10 million, Washington state $5 million, Michigan nearly $3 million, and Oklahoma more than $1 million, to legal aid organizations addressing local crime victim priorities such as domestic violence, sexual assault, elder abuse, and human trafficking.

PART II: LEGAL AID ADVANCING
FEDERAL PRIORITIES

Examples of WH-LAIR agencies' efforts in this area include:

➢ **DOJ publishes a rule for the Victims of Crime Act (VOCA) Formula Victim Assistance Grant Program to help address the unmet legal needs of crime victims.** Consistent with its 2013 Vision 21 Transforming Victim Services Report, which documented crime victims' legal needs, in 2016 DOJ's Office for Victims of Crime (OVC) published the rule for its VOCA Formula Victim Assistance Grant Program, providing greater clarity and more flexibility for state agencies to fund comprehensive legal aid among various victim services.[40]

➢ **CNCS and DOJ launch Elder Justice AmeriCorps to help elder abuse victims.** In 2016, through Elder Justice AmeriCorps, CNCS and DOJ created the first-ever army of lawyers and paralegals to help victims of elder abuse. The program will support 300 AmeriCorps members throughout the country, and grantee Equal Justice Works expects to serve more than 8,000 older adults over the next two years. To raise awareness about AmeriCorps and legal aid generally, CNCS and DOJ published the FY 2016 Guide to the AmeriCorps State and National Program for Legal Aid Organizations.

➢ **DOJ obtains legislative changes to provide legal aid to victims of domestic violence, dating violence, sexual assault, and stalking.** Prior to the passage of the Violence Against Women Reauthorization Act (VAWA) of 2013, DOJ's Office on Violence Against Women (OVW) conducted a review of VAWA programs in light of studies confirming the importance of legal aid in preventing and addressing domestic violence. The review resulted in legislation authorizing certain grant programs to allow funds to be used for legal aid, such as OVW's Rural, STOP Violence Against Women Formula Grant, and Justice for Families Programs.

➢ **DOJ's Legal Assistance for Victims (LAV) Program serves more than 25,000 victims every six months.** DOJ OVW's LAV Program helps address the critical shortage of legal services for victims of domestic violence, dating violence, sexual assault, and stalking. With LAV funding, legal aid providers obtain protection orders and address associated legal issues like divorce and child custody. LAV is one of OVW's most competitive grant programs, with more strong applications than can be funded with available resources.

➢ **HHS and DOJ fund legal aid to help human trafficking victims, and DOJ provides training and technical assistance to enhance such legal services.** HHS's Office on Trafficking in Persons funds comprehensive case management for trafficking victims and grants for victim-centered services, including legal aid. The HHS-funded National Human Trafficking Resource Center provides referrals for legal services and other resources for victims of trafficking across the country. DOJ's OVC funds legal aid for human trafficking victims through several different anti-trafficking programs,

---

Lawyer preserves essential healthcare and housing for grandmother

When 92-year-old "Sara's" health declined, she moved from assisted living to a 24-hour care nursing home. During the move it was discovered that Sara's grandson financially exploited her and that he had taken about $96,000. Because of that transfer of assets, Sara was denied Medicaid coverage for her nursing facility services, and the nursing home issued her an involuntary discharge notice. Illinois' Long Term Care Ombudsman referred Sara to LSC-funded Prairie State Legal Services. Funded in part by an HHS Older Americans Act grant, her legal aid attorney successfully appealed and obtained a Hardship Waiver from the state's Medicaid administrator so Sara could stay housed with the care she needed. Later when Sara became incapacitated, her legal aid attorney secured a state guardian to prevent further abuse by the grandson and cooperated with the criminal investigation.

PART II: LEGAL AID ADVANCING FEDERAL PRIORITIES

> *"The legal issues facing our nation's most vulnerable populations often do not fit squarely into criminal or civil boxes. And that is why the President signed a Memorandum directing the White House Legal Aid Interagency Roundtable to pull Federal agencies together to advance research and analysis of civil legal aid and indigent defense. I am confident that WH-LAIR will continue moving all of us toward a justice system that embodies respect and equality regardless of economic circumstances.*
>
> *~Roy Austin*
> *Deputy Assistant to the President for Urban Affairs, Justice, and Opportunity in Domestic Policy Council*
> *Designated WH-LAIR Co-Chair*

as well as training and technical assistance for legal aid to expand access to comprehensive legal services for victims of human trafficking and vacatur remedies for trafficking survivors.

➢ **LSC's Technology Initiative Grants (TIG) support innovative strategies to partner with police and help victims of domestic violence.** Using 2012 TIG funds, a California legal aid program created an e-filing tool for domestic violence protective order requests so that judges can issue a final order more quickly. The tool also makes the issued order available right away to the protected party as well as to police or sheriff's offices for immediate enforcement.

➢ **DOJ provides wraparound legal services to victims of crime through a demonstration project and conducts comprehensive evaluation of the project.** In 2012, DOJ's OVC launched the Wraparound Victim Legal Assistance Network Demonstration Project to develop holistic models for wraparound legal assistance networks that offer free legal assistance that victims need in the wake of their victimization. DOJ's National Institute of Justice is conducting a comprehensive independent evaluation of the project. In 2014, DOJ's OVC expanded this project to four additional sites and currently funds training and technical assistance to the legal service providers under this project.

➢ **DOJ launches initiatives to build legal aid capacity to help crime victims.** DOJ OVC's Training and Technical Assistance Center works collaboratively with national experts and offers training and technical assistance to the legal community in order to increase their knowledge base about crime victim issues and increase their capacity to provide pro bono legal representation to crime victims. Also, DOJ's Elder Justice Initiative, in collaboration with DOJ's OVC and ATJ, launched an online elder abuse training for legal aid to assist victims of elder abuse, neglect, and financial exploitation.

➢ **NSF and DOJ support the research community in identifying and seeking to fill research needs in indigent defense and access to justice.** In 2015, NSF funded a workshop on "Quality Legal Representation: Definition, Measurement, Theory and Practice." Additional white papers and new research projects continue to flow from this workshop. DOJ's NIJ has also actively supported research on indigent defense and funded projects on topics such as *Waiver of Counsel in Juvenile Court*, *Evaluating the Effect of Holistic Indigent Defense Services on Case Outcomes*, and *Examining the Effectiveness of Indigent Defense Team Services: A Multi-State Evaluation of Holistic Defense*.

➢ **State, USAID, and DOJ collaborate to promote creation of the first global network of defenders.** In May 2016, the United Nations Commission on Crime Prevention and Criminal Justice adopted a U.S.-sponsored resolution on criminal legal aid entitled, "Promoting Legal Aid, Including through a Network of Legal Aid Providers." The resolution took steps to advance practical collaboration in the criminal legal aid field, such as:

PART II: LEGAL AID ADVANCING FEDERAL PRIORITIES

(1) encouraging governments to exchange information and best practices, including on the development of national-level indicators on SDG 16 and its target 16.3, (2) endorsing the creation of national, regional, and international networks of criminal legal aid providers, and (3) inviting United Nations Member States to participate in the second international criminal legal aid conference in Argentina in November 2016. The resolution was adopted by consensus and co-sponsored by 17 countries. Efforts are underway to support implementation of the resolution.

➢ **USAID supports mapping of legal aid providers.** Through the Civil Society Innovation Initiative, part of the Stand with Civil Society Agenda, USAID supports a Global Legal Aid Mapping Project that will develop a mobile app to connect legal aid service providers with individuals and communities in need of timely legal aid representation and other legal services.

 Research says:

Police partnership with legal aid helps decrease incidence of domestic violence

The High Point Police Department partnered with LSC-funded Legal Aid of North Carolina, Family Service of the Piedmont, and other community groups to open the High Point Center for Children and Families and Victims' Justice as part of the DOJ COPS-funded Offender Focused Domestic Violence Initiative (OFDVI). OFDVI focuses on early intervention to break the cycle of domestic violence and helps victims with their civil legal needs, such as obtaining protective orders. Within the first two years of the OFVDI, recidivism rates – which typically range from 20-34% – decreased to 9% across more than 1,000 offenders.

Source: Stacy Sechrist & John Weil, *The High Point OFDVI: Preliminary Evaluation Results* (2014)

> *Research tells us that effective legal representation is the single most important factor in whether victims are able to escape this domestic violence cycle. Yet, studies estimate that less than 1 in 5 low-income victims of domestic violence ever get to see a lawyer.*
>
> ~Vice President Joe Biden

PART II: LEGAL AID ADVANCING
FEDERAL PRIORITIES

> *The Bureau has engaged legal aid groups by providing resources and technical assistance to help them better identify and address the financial challenges of their clients. Empowering consumers to successfully navigate their financial challenges may help them avoid future legal problems or the need for legal assistance.*
>
> ~Richard Cordray
> Director, CFPB

COMBATTING FRAUD AND PROTECTING CONSUMERS

Each year, approximately 25 million adults are victims of consumer fraud.[41] Victims include the poor, the elderly, and other vulnerable populations. In the worst cases, fraud can lead to homelessness and bankruptcy. The shame of being defrauded inhibits some victims from reporting scams and seeking help. Although anyone may be susceptible to abusive practices, the most vulnerable among us are often the target of mortgage scams, Ponzi schemes, abusive debt collection practices, and predatory lending schemes. In particular, older adults are targeted for their retirement savings and accumulated home equity, and because they also are more likely to experience cognitive decline, they can be more susceptible to financial scams.

Identity theft also threatens consumers. In 2015, FTC received almost half a million identity theft complaints,[42] and identity theft was included among the third most common credit card complaints made to CFPB.[43] There are over 17 million new victims annually, with devastating consequences, including tax problems, lowered credit ratings, lawsuits, and garnishment.[44] Children are also victims. A study of 40,000 children found that about 10% had someone else using their Social Security Number.[45]

Federal agencies charged with protecting consumers, such as FTC, CFPB, and DOJ, combat fraud through enforcement actions (including investigations and lawsuits) as well as educating the public on consumer protection issues. Many of these Federal programs are more effective because of partnerships with legal aid providers that help consumers assert their rights when businesses, lenders, or debt collectors have not followed the law. Legal aid can also help correct the harms caused by identity theft or credit reporting errors and can assist with reporting consumer complaints to the appropriate government agencies. Outreach and education are important strategies for legal aid to help people spot and avoid abusive tactics.[46]

WH-LAIR supports Federal agencies' efforts to combat fraud and protect consumers through strategic partnerships with legal aid in their enforcement activities and education and outreach initiatives.

Examples of WH-LAIR agencies' efforts in this area include:

- ➢ **FTC develops the Legal Services Collaboration, a nationwide and institutionalized partnership with legal aid.** In 2010, FTC launched the Legal Services Collaboration because it recognized that, by forming robust relationships with advocates for poor and underserved communities, it can more effectively fight deceptive practices affecting those communities.[47] These relationships—involving in-person or virtual meetings, regional conferences, and webinar trainings—not only inform FTC's law enforcement priorities but also allow the agency to alert local communities about scams and respond to local concerns.

PART II: LEGAL AID ADVANCING
FEDERAL PRIORITIES

- **CFPB develops a financial empowerment training toolkit for legal aid staff.** In 2015, CFPB launched Your Money, Your Goals: A financial empowerment toolkit for legal aid organizations, an interactive toolkit designed for legal aid organizations that serve low-income consumers. CFPB teamed up with four legal aid organizations from across the country to deliver workshops to train legal aid staff. In 2016, CFPB is working with additional legal aid organizations to integrate the toolkit into their work. The toolkit includes actionable information and tools for front-line staff to help clients identify financial challenges and goals, understand their consumer financial protection rights, and access relevant resources. Hundreds of legal aid attorneys and staff have participated through the train-the-trainer format via in-person and webinar trainings.

- **Treasury enlists legal aid to help low-income and other taxpayers in need with tax returns and tax disputes.** Treasury's Internal Revenue Service (IRS) administers three grant programs: Low Income Taxpayer Clinic (LITC), Volunteer Income Tax Assistance (VITA), and Tax Counseling for the Elderly (TCE). LITC funding of $12 million in FY 2016 goes to legal aid organizations and law school clinics. These programs increase access to justice by providing representation for little to no cost for low-income individuals who are trying to resolve disputes with IRS. VITA funding of $15 million in FY 2016 goes to many legal aid organizations to provide free tax return help for low-to-moderate income individuals, persons with disabilities, the elderly, and those having limited English proficiency. TCE funding of $6.5 million in FY 2016 goes to many legal aid organizations to provide free tax counseling and return preparation for the elderly. Legal aid providers also help ensure fairness and integrity in the tax system by assisting people harmed by fraudulent tax preparers.

- **HHS's Older Americans Act (OAA) funding supports legal services to senior citizens.** The Administration on Aging within the Administration for Community Living (ACL) administers OAA programs. Under the legal assistance and elder rights programs, there are about 900 OAA-funded legal aid providers nationwide providing nearly 1 million hours of legal assistance per year, such as basic will writing and estate planning as well as protection against elder abuse and financial exploitation. ACL distributed $26.6 million to civil legal aid providers for this work in FY 2014 as part of the Title III-B OAA funding. In July 2016, ACL awarded an additional $1.2 million in Model Approaches to Statewide Legal Assistance Systems demonstration grants to eight states. Grantees will expand and improve the capacity of their legal service delivery networks and improve coordination among senior legal helplines, pro bono attorneys, law school clinics, self-help sites, and OAA-funded legal aid providers, and they will promote the use of helplines and improve data collection systems. In September 2016, ACL announced release of more than $1 million to Justice in Aging to create a new National Center on Law and Elder Rights. The Center will support efforts to protect the rights, financial security and independence of older adults, and develop new resources.

> *This small sampling [of legal-aid assisted enforcement activity] shows how successful this relationship has been—and, I hope, conveys how grateful we are to work with our wonderful colleagues on the front lines of legal services to lower-income communities. They make a difference in their communities every day. We hope that, through these collaborations, the FTC helps amplify the good they do —and continues to help every consumer in every community.*
>
> ~Jessica Rich, Director, FTC Bureau of Consumer Protection

Examples of FTC Legal Services Collaboration in action:

- AARP's Legal Counsel for the Elderly referred a case to FTC about a company peddling bogus work-at-home offers. Refund checks went to 50,000 scammed consumers.

- LSC-funded Legal Aid of Arkansas reported problems with used car dealers to FTC, leading to a series of FTC undercover investigations, and resulting in warning letters to used car dealers about abuses, including for failing to display the required Buyers Guide in used cars for sale.

- LSC-funded Texas RioGrande Legal Aid identified a problem with Freedom Companies—a company supposedly offering mortgage relief services to Spanish speakers—and helped get a consumer declaration. FTC was able to shut down the business and seized all the remaining assets.

PART II: LEGAL AID ADVANCING FEDERAL PRIORITIES

 Research says:

Third-party debt collectors (acting on behalf of or in the place of the original creditor) bring at least half of all small claims cases in Maine. For a variety of reasons, the debt collectors—represented by counsel—typically prevail. Since launching a credit card debt collection project in May 2012, LSC-funded Pine Tree Legal Assistance legal aid staff and volunteer attorneys:

- represented 1,394 low-income consumers and saved clients $4,416,226 that would otherwise have been awarded to third-party debt buyers

- won more than 98% of those cases by showing that the debt collectors did not have sufficient evidence to establish the debt under Maine law

Source: Pine Tree Legal Assistance

➢ **FTC's educational video on debt collection features legal aid interventions for military families.** As part of its education and outreach about special rights servicemembers and their families have on some consumer issues, FTC's Fraud Affects Every Community: Debt Collection video tells the moving first-person story of a veteran's debt collection experience spotlighting the legal assistance that helped him recover.

➢ **FTC partners with legal aid to develop and disseminate consumer education and to track complaints from certain legal aid offices.** FTC recently developed a pilot program to help select legal aid offices file consumer complaints more easily with FTC's Consumer Sentinel database and to increase dissemination of consumer education materials. New complaints will be automatically tagged as originating from a legal aid program, which will enable the FTC to measure the number and type of consumer complaints coming from these offices. FTC also utilized its legal aid partnership to develop Consumer.gov, which presents easy-to-use information through text, videos, presentations, and worksheets.

➢ **Treasury raises awareness about the role for legal aid in financial education through the Financial Literacy and Education Commission (FLEC).** On June 29, 2016, the WH-LAIR Executive Director, WH-LAIR representatives from CFPB and FTC, and a legal aid attorney addressed FLEC's 22 member agencies and other participants about partnering with legal aid to further FLEC's work of helping people achieve their financial goals and attain greater financial stability in their lives.

PART II: LEGAL AID ADVANCING FEDERAL PRIORITIES

MEETING THE NEEDS OF SPECIAL POPULATIONS: VETERANS AND SERVICEMEMBERS, TRIBES AND TRIBAL MEMBERS, PEOPLE WITH DISABILITIES, PEOPLE WITH CRIMINAL RECORDS, IMMIGRANTS, AND DISASTER SURVIVORS

Certain populations face unique or greater barriers to access to justice, and WH-LAIR agencies are responding to their needs by providing targeted services, including legal aid. This section provides additional context for those populations and briefly describes efforts to meet their needs.

VETERANS AND SERVICEMEMBERS

Many of the more than 21 million American veterans and another 1.4 million servicemembers face serious challenges, including unemployment, chronic health problems, and homelessness. On a single night in January 2015, nearly 48,000 veterans experienced homelessness.[48] Veterans face a housing crisis for many reasons, such as poverty, lack of support from family or friends, or substance use disorders or mental health conditions that may have developed or worsened as a result of trauma they experienced while serving. Many of our servicemembers and veterans need access to physical and behavioral health services, critical income supports, and especially job opportunities when they return to civilian life.

VA and other Federal agencies coordinate their resources to assist veterans, servicemembers, and their families in need. A growing number of these programs include legal aid because legal aid is often necessary to meet veterans' and servicemembers' essential and otherwise unmet needs. Through representation, counseling, and education, legal aid helps prevent evictions and home foreclosures. For child support issues, legal aid helps negotiate fair child support orders, increasing the reliability of payments. Additionally, legal aid helps veterans navigate outstanding warrants and court fines and fees, and can help restore a revoked or suspended driver's license, which is often necessary for work. Veterans who need help securing government benefits can receive assistance from legal aid, ensuring that applications are completed correctly and, if a veteran's benefits are erroneously terminated, help reinstate the benefits by working with the agency or representing the veteran in administrative proceedings.[49]

WH-LAIR helps Federal agencies identify those programs that can be more effective by incorporating legal aid among the services that they offer to veterans and servicemembers and increase collaboration and sharing of best practices, such as exchanges between HHS and VA about their experiences improving health outcomes through medical-legal partnerships.

> *Steady progress has been made, but there is more work to do to address the many causes of homelessness among Veterans. Providing legal aid to remove obstacles to stable housing, such as helping to address eviction or foreclosure, is a critical part of this effort.*
>
> *~Robert A. McDonald*
> *Secretary, VA*

PART II: LEGAL AID ADVANCING FEDERAL PRIORITIES

Hospital's legal triage keeps roof over veteran's head

When "Clyde" sought medical help from the Philadelphia VA Medical Center, a social worker learned he had fallen behind on his rent and faced eviction from his apartment. The social worker and the SSVF caseworker recognized Clyde's need for legal help and connected Clyde with an attorney at the SSVF program's legal aid partner, Homeless Advocacy Project. With the SSVF program providing some of Clyde's back rent, the attorney negotiated an agreement to stop the eviction in exchange for a lump sum payment for most of the unpaid rent, plus a payment plan to cover the remainder. With his housing stabilized, Clyde was able to focus on his health needs.

Examples of WH-LAIR agencies' efforts in this area include:

- **DOL funds legal aid through grants from its Veterans' Employment and Training Service (VETS).** The DOL VETS-funded Homeless Veterans' Reintegration Program grant allows the use of grant funds for legal aid in the areas of family law, domestic violence, child support enforcement, and credit repair counseling, to support eligible homeless female veterans and veterans with families.

- **VA issues guidance supporting veterans' access to legal aid at VA medical facilities.** VA issued a Directive in 2011 and a Policy Memorandum in 2012 to Office of General Counsel attorneys on advising VA facilities and on how to refer homeless veterans to legal service providers for assistance with matters such as child support or outstanding warrants or fines, and to provide office space to legal service providers, when possible. As of September 2016, there were over 135 free legal clinics operating in VA medical facilities nationwide, including 12 medical-legal partnerships, a more than 300 percent increase since 2012. VA now tracks the growth of these clinics and provides legal and other technical guidance to the local VA staff coordinating these clinics.[50]

- **VA provides training to its program staff and grantees about the legal needs of homeless veterans and partners with HHS to provide legal help to homeless veterans.** VA, in collaboration with DOJ and legal aid programs, provided training about the legal needs of veterans and how to incorporate legal services into efforts to help veterans obtain permanent housing.[51] This effort included a webinar series in 2015 to all grantees of the Supportive Services for Veteran Families (SSVF) program on housing-related legal interventions and a training event in 2016 to the Grant per Diem program staff. In addition, VA, HHS's Office of Child Support Enforcement, and the American Bar Association piloted a nine-site partnership to provide homeless veterans with help addressing child support debt.

- **DOJ launches the Servicemembers and Veterans Initiative (Initiative) to build a comprehensive legal support network focused on protecting servicemembers, veterans, and military family members.** Launched in 2015, the Initiative's engagement efforts include www.servicemembers.gov, a new website designed to educate servicemembers and legal professionals about the military-specific Federal statutes enforced by DOJ and features a form that serves as an effective means by which servicemembers and veterans may bring legal issues to the attention of DOJ.

- **VA initiates VA-accredited legal aid attorneys' electronic access to veteran clients' claim records.** In 2016, VA began actively processing requests from VA-accredited attorneys for electronic access to veteran clients' claim records. Previously, the electronic access to records was only available to the representatives of VA-recognized Veterans Service Organizations.

PART II: LEGAL AID ADVANCING FEDERAL PRIORITIES

➢ **VA is actively pursuing improvements to its hearings and appeals process for veterans' benefits.** VA included a proposal in the 2017 President's Budget for a more streamlined appeals process, setting a goal of most veterans receiving a final appeals decision within one year of filing their appeal. Many veterans receive free assistance with their claims and appeals from VA-recognized Veterans Service Organizations, and VA is exploring options for expanding access to those and other legal aid organizations.

➢ **FCC adopted a comprehensive reform and modernization of the Lifeline program.** Lifeline provides a discount on phone service for qualifying low-income consumers to ensure they have the ability to connect to jobs, information, and emergency services. In March 2016, FCC modified its rules to grant eligibility for Lifeline to low-income consumers receiving the Veterans Pension benefit or the Survivors Pension benefit. The program will also begin supporting a discount on fixed and mobile broadband internet access service in December 2016. FCC will perform outreach to legal aid organizations to ensure veteran clients are aware of the program.

TRIBES AND TRIBAL MEMBERS

The Federal government's relationship with, and responsibility to, members of Federally-recognized Indian tribes is long and complex, governed by treaties, court decisions, a multitude of Federal laws, and executive orders. Together, these affect many aspects of life for tribal members, including child custody, estate planning, healthcare, and education.

As a consequence of the historical practice of removing Native American children from their families for placement with non-Native families, Congress enacted the Indian Child Welfare Act (ICWA). Although the law created safeguards to preserve families, it is difficult to navigate without legal assistance. The same is true for the preparation of Indian wills, which is complex because tribal lands are held in trust by the Federal government.

Moreover, many tribes enact their own laws to establish law and order on their lands, adding to the need for lawyers with specialized knowledge of Federal and tribal laws and practices. This specialized legal knowledge has become more important after the passage of the Violence Against Women Reauthorization Act of 2013 (VAWA 2013) and the newly recognized Special Domestic Violence Criminal Jurisdiction and its requirement for more robust tribal defender services.

Legal aid helps preserve Native American families by assisting tribes in developing and implementing social programs and by representing parents in cases that implicate ICWA. Legal aid helps tribal members secure Federal benefits by helping individuals enroll in their tribe and receive health and social services such as Social Security benefits, disability payments, and Indian Health Service benefits. Legal aid also helps protect land rights of Native Americans by helping to prepare wills to protect family property rights and representing tribal members in actions to protect their hunting and fishing rights on tribal land. In addition, legal aid assists tribal members in tribal courts by providing representation to low-income criminal defendants and juveniles in delinquency proceedings.[52]

 Research says:

5 of the top 10 unmet needs of homeless veterans involve legal assistance for: eviction/foreclosure prevention, child support issues, outstanding warrants/fines, discharge upgrades, and restoring a driver's license. Other top 10 unmet needs often have a legal component, including family reconciliation assistance and credit counseling.

Source: U.S. Dep't of Veterans Affairs, Community Homelessness Assessment, Local Education and Networking Groups Fact Sheet (2016).

"*Indian communities are plagued by high rates of poverty, and a multitude of unmet legal needs. Legal aid can play a vital role in ensuring safety, stability, and economic security for tribal members.*

~Kevin Washburn
former Assistant Secretary
Indian Affairs, DOI

PART II: LEGAL AID ADVANCING FEDERAL PRIORITIES

Doctor prescribes a lawyer to keep Navajo family healthy and housed

After "Rose," a citizen of the Navajo Nation, lost her adult daughter in a car accident, she was left to raise five grandchildren. With no room for the children in her own house, Rose moved into her deceased daughter's apartment. Still grieving, Rose received an eviction notice from the housing agency, because she was not named on the apartment lease. They told her that she and the children had to move. When a pediatrician at the Indian Health Service clinic learned of the situation, she referred Rose to DNA-People's Legal Services Medical-Legal Partnership Program, funded by LSC and DOJ's Tribal Civil Legal Assistance Program. With the help of her DNA-People's Legal Services lawyer, Rose showed that tribal law and Federal policies allowed her to assume the lease obligations. Rose continued to care for the children in their own home and, with DNA's help, obtained legal guardianship over each grandchild.

Examples of WH-LAIR agencies' efforts in this area include:

➢ **LSC-funded programs work in Indian Country and in urban areas where Native Americans are concentrated to provide specialized legal aid.** These programs provide highly skilled legal services in the complex body of Indian law to address critical needs such as child custody in Indian Child Welfare Act (ICWA) cases and probate matters under the American Indian Probate Reform Act. Some programs also provide defense services in tribal courts.

➢ **DOI provides free legal training in tribal courts.** DOI's Bureau of Indian Affairs (BIA) helps fund and support 184 tribal courts and provides free trainings designed to strengthen the trial skills of tribal judges, prosecutors, and defenders. Since the enactment of VAWA 2013 and the newly recognized Special Domestic Violence Criminal Jurisdiction, BIA has supported additional tribal court trainings led by tribes that have begun implementing the law. Since 2016, DOI has provided additional training to tribal court personnel, including legal aid providers, on domestic violence protection orders pursuant to VAWA 2013 and child welfare hearings in Public Law 280 jurisdictions, such as Alaska and California.[53]

➢ **CNCS launches medical-legal partnerships (MLPs) in Indian Country.** CNCS serves Native American communities through a number of programs including AmeriCorps. In 2015, CNCS awarded an AmeriCorps Indian Tribes Planning Grant to a partnership among the Navajo Nation, the Kenaitze Indian Tribe, the Central Council of Tlingit and Haida, and the Tanana Chiefs Conference, in conjunction with two legal aid programs to develop MLPs in Indian Country. Subsequently in 2016, the partnership was awarded an operational grant.

➢ **DOJ's Tribal Civil and Criminal Legal Assistance program (TCCLA) supports civil and criminal legal aid to Native Americans.** Administered by DOJ's Bureau of Justice Assistance (BJA), TCCLA provides grants to 26 legal aid programs to represent low-income Native Americans in civil matters, such as housing, and criminal cases involving violations of tribal criminal law. TCCLA also supports core training and technical assistance for legal aid staff, peacemaking approaches and curriculum development and training on holistic representation approaches. Also sponsored by BJA, the Tribal Access to Justice Innovation website highlights innovative tribal justice programs from around the country in an effort to provide ideas to reformers looking to address common challenges.

➢ **DOJ supports legal aid to address domestic violence among tribal members.** Through the Coordinated Tribal Assistance Solicitation, BJA and the Office on Violence Against Women (OVW) provide funding to tribes for legal aid to low-income tribal members to address domestic violence. Additionally, in 2016, OVW launched a new program, Grants to Tribal Governments to Exercise Special Domestic Violence Criminal Jurisdiction Program, to support tribal governments' exercise of VAWA 2013's Special Domestic Violence Criminal Jurisdiction. In September 2016, OVW announced that it is awarding $2.1 million to seven tribes under this program. Through this program, OVW for the first time can fund the provision of criminal defense services for low-income individuals charged with domestic violence and dating violence, as well as violating certain protection orders.

➢ **DOI's Bureau of Indian Affairs (BIA) funds tribal efforts to provide legal aid for their members.** Over the years, BIA has provided funding to support legal aid in tribal communities through base funding, one-time funding, and court improvement funding. For example, in 2016 BIA provided continuous base funding for legal aid to the following tribes: Red Lake, Spirit Lake, Pueblo of Pojoaque, Makah, Eastern Band of Cherokee, Ft. Belknap, Pueblo of Isleta, Rosebud Sioux, and Pascua Yaqui.

➢ **FCC maintains tribal-specific Lifeline eligibility programs to support adoption of telecommunications services.** Low-income consumers living on tribal lands and receiving certain Federally funded benefits are eligible for a $34.25 discount on phone service. Beginning in December 2016, the Lifeline program will also support fixed and mobile broadband internet access services for qualifying tribal households. With this benefit, tribal members can maintain contact with legal counsel and increase their access to online information and resources.

➢ **HUD's Indian Housing Block Grant (IHBG) program funds affordable housing development and related housing services including legal services.** The IHBG funds, provided through Indian tribes and tribally designated housing entities, may be used to provide housing-related legal services to low-income residents of affordable housing and persons seeking affordable housing assistance.

PEOPLE WITH DISABILITIES

Many of the over 50 million Americans with disabilities face serious challenges that impact their basic needs. Although the nature and severity of disabilities and associated challenges vary, those with disabilities experience unemployment, poverty, lack of access to health services, discrimination, and difficulty accessing appropriate educational services more often than those without a disability.

The Federal government has long recognized the importance of legal aid in addressing challenges faced by Americans with disabilities. Through the Protection and Advocacy System (P&A) programs, funded by several Federal agencies, many Americans with disabilities receive critical legal assistance. Specifically, the legal aid providers from P&A and other programs help prevent or stop discrimination and enforce rights in employment, government services, public accommodations, housing, and school. Legal aid also helps secure government benefits such as Social Security, Medicaid, and veterans' benefits, by explaining eligibility requirements, properly documenting applications, helping to waive unjust overpayment demands, and appealing erroneous denials, terminations, and reductions. Additionally, those with disabilities can receive help ensuring that housing and workplaces are accessible.[54]

> *Legal aid plays a vital role in serving Americans with disabilities and creating a stable living environment for the most vulnerable people in our society.*
>
> ~Carolyn W. Colvin
> Acting Commissioner of Social Security

PART II: LEGAL AID ADVANCING
FEDERAL PRIORITIES

> **P&A lawyer listens to teacher's tale of denial of services for hearing loss**
>
> When "Jack" realized his already limited hearing had deteriorated, he knew he needed new hearing aids to keep his teaching job. But when Jack requested a replacement device, Indiana Vocational Rehabilitation Services (VR), the state government office that helps people with disabilities get and retain employment, denied the request because VR's policy required a hearing change of at least 10 decibels to provide replacement devices and Jack didn't meet that requirement. Indiana Protection and Advocacy Services (IPAS), with funding from the Department of Education's Client Assistant Program, appealed the denial. At the appeal, the administrative law judge determined that VR's 10-decibel requirement was inconsistent with Federal law, as it did not account for the individual needs of each VR client. Thanks to IPAS's help, Jack received new hearing aids and kept his job. IPAS also used the decision to help other Hoosiers needing replacement hearing aids to retain their employment.

WH-LAIR supports Federal agencies' strategic partnerships with civil legal aid to assist programs that target Americans with disabilities and to aid the enforcement of key Federal and state laws protecting the rights of Americans with disabilities.

Examples of WH-LAIR agencies' efforts in this area include:

- **HHS, ED, and SSA provide legal aid to persons with disabilities through the P&A programs.** P&A programs provide legal representation and other advocacy services to persons with disabilities, including individuals with developmental disabilities, mental illness and other impairments such as visual or hearing impairments.[55] In FY 2015, these programs provided advocacy services to over 45,000 individuals and information and referral services to over 141,000 individuals.

- **HHS, ED, and SSA partner with the National Disability Rights Network (NDRN) to provide technical assistance to P&A programs providing legal aid.** NDRN, a nonprofit membership organization for P&A programs, provides training and technical assistance to those P&A programs through contracts with SSA, ED and HHS.

- **DOJ partners with legal aid and P&A programs in enforcement actions to protect the legal rights of people with disabilities.** Many of the enforcement cases brought by DOJ's Civil Rights Division begin as referrals from legal aid organizations or P&A programs. In other cases, DOJ has intervened or filed statements of interest to support litigation brought by legal aid providers seeking to increase accessibility and ensure appropriate placements and services for people with disabilities.

- **SSA starts Pre-Hearing Conference Pilot Program for self-represented claimants.** Under this program, senior attorneys in SSA's Office of Disability Adjudication and Review conduct pre-hearing conferences with self-represented claimants to explain the hearing process and right to a representative and obtain updated records information in preparation for the formal hearing. The goals for the pre-hearing conference are to (1) reduce hearing no-shows and postponements based on a claimant choosing to seek representation, (2) improve the quality and completeness of the record at the time of the hearing, and (3) decrease the need for post-hearing development and improve the hearings experience for self-represented claimants.

- **SSA supports research on disability-related topics, including legal aid.** SSA administers the Disability Determination Process Small Grant Program, and several projects in this program address the role of legal services in assisting claimants with the disability application process. Also, SSA contracted with ACUS to study state adult guardianship laws and court practices concerning the selection, monitoring, and sanctioning of legal guardians. ACUS released its findings in 2015.[56]

PART II: LEGAL AID ADVANCING
FEDERAL PRIORITIES

PEOPLE WITH CRIMINAL RECORDS

Each year, more than 600,000 individuals are released from state and Federal prisons, and 11.4 million people cycle through local jails.[57] In addition, a broader population – roughly one in three American adults – has an arrest record, many for relatively minor, non-violent offenses, sometimes from decades in the past or as a result of their mental health conditions.[58] The long-term, sometimes lifetime, impact of a criminal record keeps many qualified people from obtaining employment and accessing housing, higher education, loans and credit—even after they have paid their debt to society.

As a number of Federal programs strive to support those with criminal records with the myriad challenges they face, partnership with legal aid is essential. For example, legal aid can secure expungement or sealing of records or even a pardon for eligible people, thereby improving prospects for employment, housing, and education. Legal aid can also correct errors on criminal records, reinstate a revoked or suspended driver's license, and modify child support orders to realistic payment obligations, helping parents provide for their families.[59]

WH-LAIR collaborates with the Federal Interagency Reentry Council, which coordinates Federal agencies' efforts around reentry, to ensure that legal aid is among the range of services provided by those Federal programs designed to tackle barriers for individuals with criminal records.

Examples of WH-LAIR agencies' efforts in this area include:

> *We are a nation that believes in second chances. Providing legal services to help individuals make a successful transition back to their communities, while also empowering them with the skills necessary to find a good job and thrive in the workplace, will help strengthen our economy and our society.*
>
> ~Thomas Perez
> Secretary, DOL

- **DOJ sponsors post-disposition reentry fellowships.** Funded by the Second Chance Act, DOJ's Office of Juvenile Justice and Delinquency Prevention (OJJDP) awardee National Juvenile Defender Center selected four organizations to host reentry fellows. These fellows provide post-disposition civil legal services to address barriers youth face in community reintegration following a juvenile delinquency placement or commitment. Legal aid may include juvenile record expungement, securing a driver's license, challenging inappropriate denials of housing or employment, educational advocacy, and other services that help youth successfully reenter the community.

- **HUD and DOJ help youth in public housing with collateral consequences associated with a juvenile or criminal record.** With funding from DOJ's OJJDP, in 2016, HUD provided 21 Juvenile Reentry Assistance Program (JRAP) grants to provide legal aid to eligible public housing residents under the age of 25. JRAP services include assistance with expunging, sealing, or correcting juvenile or adult records as permitted by state law and supportive services to assist with mitigating and/or preventing collateral consequences.

PART II: LEGAL AID ADVANCING
FEDERAL PRIORITIES

Lawyer's help gets a nurse on the job

"Andy's" 10-year-old felony conviction prevented him from pursuing his hopes of securing a state license to become a New York Licensed Practical Nurse. The Fortune Society, a grantee of DOL's Reentry Employment Opportunities grant program, referred Andy to MFY Legal Services in New York. His legal aid lawyer helped Andy obtain out-of-state criminal court records, gather proof of rehabilitation, and represented him at the initial investigative interview. The result was a successful license application and a job.

➢ **DOL and DOJ establish the National Clean Slate Clearinghouse.** In September 2016, the DOL and DOJ announced a partnership with the Council of State Governments Justice Center to establish the National Clean Slate Clearinghouse to provide technical assistance to local legal aid programs, public defender offices, and reentry service providers to build capacity for legal aid needed to help with record-cleaning, expungement, and related civil legal services.

➢ **DOJ and DOL expand legal aid to address collateral consequences for people with criminal records.** Several large grant programs – such as the DOJ Second Chance Act grants, DOL Reentry Employment Opportunities grants, and HHS Child Support Noncustodial Parents Employment Demonstration grants – allow for the use of funds to pay for legal assistance to secure driver's licenses, expunge criminal records, modify child support orders, and litigate inappropriate denials of housing or employment and violations of the Fair Credit Reporting Act for people returning to their communities from a period of incarceration.

IMMIGRANTS

People need quality legal representation in immigration proceedings. Legal aid groups play a valuable role in filling that need. They help people navigate a complicated process and help immigration courts function more effectively and efficiently.

~Juan Osuna
Director
DOJ Executive Office for
Immigration Review

Many individuals who appear before immigration courts are indigent and cannot afford a private attorney. According to DOJ's Executive Office for Immigration Review (EOIR), over 40 percent of the individuals in immigration proceedings are without legal representation at the time of their initial case completions.[60] In addition to the complexity of immigration law, many unrepresented litigants lack English language proficiency or any knowledge of the American legal system. A recent study of over 1.2 million immigration cases from between 2007 and 2012 demonstrates that immigrants with legal representation are more likely to apply for immigration relief and are more likely to obtain the relief they sought.[61]

Unfamiliarity with the American legal system makes immigrants especially vulnerable to the unauthorized practice of immigration law, also known as notario fraud — a form of consumer fraud that involves individuals who misrepresent themselves as qualified to provide immigration legal services. Victims of notario fraud can suffer significant consequences, including delay of their applications or petitions, paying unnecessary and costly fees, and even the risk of jeopardizing their immigration status and removal.

Civil legal aid lawyers provide legal representation or advice to those who cannot afford a private attorney in immigration proceedings, including the most vulnerable immigrant populations such as unaccompanied children and those with serious mental disorders or conditions. These lawyers help people navigate the immigration system and access appropriate social services and assist lawful permanent residents with the naturalization application and interview processes. In addition, legal aid protects immigrants from notario fraud by providing them with information and resources to better understand immigration proceedings and by assisting them with correcting their filings. Immigrants who are victims of crime can also receive help from legal aid to apply for U or T nonimmigrant status, which is available to eligible victims of crimes such as domestic violence and human trafficking.

Recognizing the vulnerability of many immigrants and the need for legal help, WH-LAIR agencies provide various resources, including legal aid.

Examples of WH-LAIR agencies' efforts in this area include:

- **FTC, DOJ, and DHS form a multi-agency, nationwide initiative to combat immigration services scams.** This initiative, launched in 2011, targets immigration scams involving the unauthorized practice of immigration law and focuses on enforcement, education and continued collaboration. As part of the initiative, FTC collects complaints in order to detect patterns of wrongdoing. The initiative implemented programs designed to help those in immigration proceedings, including DOJ EOIR's "Know Your Rights" trainings at detention centers and DHS's "The Wrong Help Can Hurt" campaign aimed at preventing notario fraud.

- **CNCS and DOJ launch justice AmeriCorps to increase legal aid to unrepresented immigrant children who have crossed the U.S. border without a parent or legal guardian.** The justice AmeriCorps program, launched in 2014, enrolled approximately 70 lawyers and paralegals in each of the past two years as AmeriCorps members to provide legal aid to the most vulnerable of these children, responding to Congress' direction to better serve vulnerable populations, such as children, and improve court efficiency through pilot efforts aimed at improving legal representation. justice AmeriCorps provides direct representation through a grant model to certain unaccompanied minors[62] in immigration removal proceedings at 20 immigration courts across the country. Through August 2016, justice AmeriCorps members have accepted over 2,300 cases.

- **DHS awards grants to legal aid programs, among others, to help with citizenship preparation for lawful permanent residents.** As part of a multifaceted effort to provide citizenship preparation resources, support, and information to lawful permanent residents and immigrant-serving organizations, DHS's U.S. Citizenship and Immigration Services (USCIS) runs the Citizenship and Integration Grant Program, which has provided funding since 2009 to make citizenship instruction and naturalization application services accessible to the low-income and other underserved lawful permanent resident populations. The grant program has awarded 308 competitive grants to numerous organizations in 37 states.

---

justice AmeriCorps lawyer gets asylum for young crime victim

When 14-year-old "Paulo" was shot and severely beaten by a gang member in his native El Salvador, he knew he had to leave his grandparents' home where he had lived much of his life. Paulo vigorously denied the gang's claim that his family belonged to a rival gang, an accusation equivalent to a death sentence in his community. Arriving in the United States alone, a Catholic Charities of Rockville Center justice AmeriCorps Fellow took Paulo's case and successfully represented him in removal proceedings before the New York Immigration Court. Granted asylum, Paulo was reunited with his parents. The justice AmeriCorps partnership with Catholic Charities enabled Paulo to also get a Social Security card and mental health counseling to address his trauma, helping him settle into his new life as an eighth grader with a key position on his church's soccer team.

PART II: LEGAL AID ADVANCING FEDERAL PRIORITIES

- **DOJ supports initiatives to ensure the fairness and accessibility of administrative justice for those without legal representation.** EOIR, through its Legal Orientation Program (LOP), provides in-person orientations, self-help assistance, and pro bono referrals to individuals detained by the U.S. Immigration and Customs Enforcement (ICE). Using contracted non-profit legal service providers, LOP currently operates in 36 of the largest or most actively utilized ICE detention facilities and has two smaller programs servicing non-detained individuals. EOIR also provides similar services to custodians of unaccompanied minor children released from the custody of HHS's Administration for Children and Families, Office of Refugee Resettlement's Unaccompanied Children Program. EOIR also recently launched the Immigration Court Helpdesk Program (ICH) which funds information helpdesks at five immigration courts with some of the greatest pending caseloads and longest backlogs.

- **DOJ launches innovative pilot programs that provide representation to certain vulnerable populations.** The National Qualified Representative Program, overseen by EOIR since 2014, provides representation to unrepresented individuals detained by ICE and found by an immigration judge to be mentally incompetent to represent themselves in immigration proceedings. EOIR also funds the Baltimore Representation Initiative for Unaccompanied Children (BRIUC) to provide direct representation in immigration proceedings to certain unaccompanied children appearing before the Baltimore Immigration Court. In addition, in 2015 EOIR established the Remote Access Initiative (RAI), which funds legal representation for certain unaccompanied children in immigration removal proceedings before the Memphis Immigration Court who would not otherwise be represented by counsel due to their geographic distance from the court and legal services.

- **HHS facilitates legal aid for unaccompanied immigrant children.** HHS's Administration for Children and Families, Office for Refugee Resettlement (ORR), through its legal service providers, conducts legal screenings for unaccompanied immigrant children to determine their potential eligibility for immigration relief. ORR also supports pro bono legal representation and funds legal representation for certain unaccompanied children. In addition, ORR provides "Know Your Rights" presentations, information regarding the availability of free legal assistance and notices to unaccompanied children of their eligibility to apply for Special Immigrant Juvenile Status.

- **DHS establishes legal access coordinator and subject matter expert positions to enhance legal aid to detained immigrants.** Beginning in 2016, these new positions in ICE help improve and implement legal access protocols, engage stakeholders at the national and local levels, and coordinate with interagency partners and nongovernmental organizations, as appropriate, to enhance "know-your-rights" presentations and EOIR-funded legal orientation programs to detained immigrants.

PART II: LEGAL AID ADVANCING
FEDERAL PRIORITIES

- ➢ **ED creates a website of educational resources for immigrants, refugees, asylees, and other new Americans.** The website contains resources that support a number of immigrant populations, including immigrant children (e.g., unaccompanied youth) and the children of immigrants, Deferred Action for Childhood Arrivals children and youth, immigrant families, adult immigrants (e.g. refugees, asylees), migrant students, teachers of English learners and foreign languages, and receiving communities. The website includes information on legal rights and is geared toward students, teachers, schools and communities to support civic, economic, and linguistic integration.

- ➢ **DOJ works to ensure comprehensive language assistance services in state courts for limited English proficiency (LEP) individuals.** DOJ's Civil Rights Division has worked with state courts to improve their programs, including through collaborative cooperation, investigations, and enforcement efforts, so that LEP individuals have greater access to the court system.[63]

DISASTER SURVIVORS

Disasters can hit anywhere and at any time. They can be caused by natural hazards, such as tornados, hurricanes, volcanic eruptions, and floods, or be human-induced, such as environmental disasters or terrorism. When disaster strikes, women, children and people with disabilities are especially vulnerable to death, job loss, and housing insecurity, but much can be done to mitigate the impacts of disasters.

Legal aid providers help protect lives and livelihoods, addressing matters critical to alleviating the devastating effects of a disaster. Almost immediately after a disaster, survivors typically need advice and counsel regarding evictions, price-gouging, eligibility for disaster-related benefits such as Individual Disaster Assistance, Disaster SNAP, Disaster Unemployment Assistance, and Federal Housing Administration (FHA) insurance issues, and help replacing legal identification papers. Later, many will need help with insurance claims regarding loss of property and loss of life, bankruptcy, foreclosures, heir property and title concerns, preparing new wills and other legal papers that were destroyed, tax issues, combating consumer fraud, and family law matters such as child custody and guardianship issues.

> *Civil legal aid providers are valued whole community partners who play an integral role in helping disaster survivors recover and rebuild.*
>
> ~W. Craig Fugate
> Administrator
> DHS Federal Emergency Management Agency

Understanding the role of legal aid in meeting the short- and long-term needs of disaster survivors, WH-LAIR agencies have taken various steps to include legal aid in the services they provide to this vulnerable population.

Examples of WH-LAIR agencies' efforts in this area include:

- ➢ **DHS's Federal Emergency Management Administration (FEMA) partners with the American Bar Association to provide legal aid to disaster survivors.** When the President declares a disaster, FEMA, through an

PART II: LEGAL AID ADVANCING FEDERAL PRIORITIES

> **Legal aid helps family rebuild their home and lives**
>
> When Hurricane Sandy raged through Staten Island in October 2012, it badly damaged the home of "Mr. and Mrs. Porto," where they lived with their son and Mr. Porto's elderly father. It also wiped out the income from Mr. Porto's auto detailing business, leaving them with income only from Mrs. Porto's housekeeping work. As the family struggled to get back on their feet, Legal Services NYC (LSNYC) —thanks to a LSC grant made available by the Disaster Relief Appropriations Act—helped them successfully challenge an insurance underpayment so they could repair their roof and blown-out windows. Their income loss left them unable to keep up with their monthly mortgage payments, so they requested and received some loan forbearance. But when the mortgage company demanded full payment of more than $17,000 in suspended payments, the Portos did not have the lump sum, and the mortgage company began foreclosure. LSNYC represented the Portos and successfully settled the dispute by securing a loan modification to an amount they could afford, enabling the Portos to save their home and rebuild their lives.

agreement with the Young Lawyers Division of the American Bar Association, mobilizes local legal aid and pro bono volunteers to provide free legal help for disaster survivors through the request of the state, local, tribal, or territorial government. This program, Disaster Legal Services, provides legal assistance to low-income individuals who, prior to or because of the disaster, are unable to secure legal aid to meet their disaster-related needs. This program expands the scope of available legal services for disaster survivors by providing assistance to a broader audience than that typically provided by legal aid because of its more flexible low-income standard and lack of immigration status restrictions.

➢ **DHS's FEMA issues a guide on disaster recovery and identified legal services as an unmet need to be addressed.** FEMA's National Disaster Recovery Framework, a guide on how the whole community builds, sustains, and coordinates delivery of recovery capabilities to meet the needs of affected community members who have experienced the hardships of financial, emotional, and/or physical impacts of devastating disasters, notes that typical areas of unmet need include legal services and that legal services should be included in a successful recovery plan.

➢ **LSC provides funding to build the National Disaster Legal Aid website.** In 2012, LSC provided a Technology Initiative Grant to Lone Star Legal Aid to rebuild and enhance the National Disaster Legal Aid website, which now serves as a centralized national resource for legal aid and pro bono attorneys on legal issues related to all types of disasters, as well as a platform to recruit and mobilize volunteer attorneys following a disaster. The website also provides timely legal information to help low- and moderate-income people with their disaster-related legal issues.

➢ **HUD, DOJ, DHS, HHS, and DOT issue joint guidance about protecting civil rights of those affected by disasters and urge partnership with legal aid.** In 2016, five agencies jointly issued guidance to assist recipients of Federal funding engaged in emergency management to ensure that individuals and communities affected by disasters do not face unlawful discrimination on the basis of race, color, or national origin (including limited English proficiency) in violation of Title VI of the Civil Rights Act of 1964. Noting that legal aid organizations are trusted intermediaries that can engage with underserved communities, the guidance urges recipients to consider working with legal aid organizations before, during, and after an emergency or disaster.

➢ **LSC helps Hurricane Sandy survivors with legal needs.** The Disaster Relief Appropriations Act of 2013 included $1 million for LSC to provide assistance to low-income people in areas significantly affected by Hurricane Sandy. The grants—which were supplemented by more than $1 million from private foundations—funded legal aid needed for low-income families, seniors, veterans, and others to recover and rebuild their lives following the disaster.

PART III: LOOKING AHEAD

Accelerating WH-LAIR Activities and Amplifying Their Impact

"Civil legal aid can transform lives for the better, and WH-LAIR is committed to helping provide these critical services, building on the efforts of the last four years to meet the challenges ahead.

*~Principal Deputy Associate Attorney General Bill Baer
Designated WH-LAIR Co-Chair*

Much has been accomplished, but so much more can be done to improve the performance of Federal programs by ensuring meaningful access to justice for all in America. WH-LAIR agencies have demonstrated that civil legal aid is an essential but often underfunded and underutilized partner, and they intend, where appropriate, to add legal aid into the mix of policy responses to the problems they seek to solve. During the year since the Presidential Memorandum was signed, WH-LAIR agencies have both taken stock of the progress they have made to date and begun to plan the activities that will accelerate and amplify their efforts going forward.

➤ **Leveraging resources to strengthen Federal programs by integrating legal aid.** WH-LAIR agencies will continue to leverage Federal funding and training and technical assistance (TTA) opportunities to include legal aid. Notable examples include: DOL is reviewing all of its funding competitions to determine whether legal aid should be included among the services provided; DOJ will continue providing TTA to encourage its grantees to fund more comprehensive legal assistance for crime victims; CFPB will provide TTA to select legal aid programs to expand the reach of its financial empowerment toolkit, *Your Money, Your Goals*; and DOJ's FY 2017 budget request includes $5 million for a competitive grant program for states to create integrated civil legal aid delivery systems to better meet the legal needs of low- and moderate-income people and reduce the caseload burden on courts.

➤ **Developing and implementing policy recommendations that improve access to justice.** WH-LAIR agencies plan to develop a broader range of policies that further the goals of WH-LAIR and work towards effective implementation of their new policies. For example, HHS's Children's Bureau at the Administration for Children and Families is developing guidance to emphasize and promote the importance of high quality legal representation for all parties in all stages of child welfare proceedings; HHS's Office of Child Support Enforcement has proposed a rule that would support services to improve access to court hearings and other adjudicative processes for people without lawyers; and DOL will implement its recently published WIOA final rules and provide jobseekers with the supportive services they need—including legal aid—to secure employment.

PART II: LEGAL AID ADVANCING FEDERAL PRIORITIES

The dozen agencies in the Working Group on Self-Represented Parties in Administrative Hearings continue to explore promising practices for hearing procedures to ensure the fairness and accuracy of administrative decisions that affect vital public benefits. As co-chair, ACUS plans to finalize its draft report and recommendations based on its review of available data and research for agencies that conduct administrative hearings in late 2016.

➢ **Facilitating strategic partnerships to achieve enforcement and outreach objectives.** Learning from the enforcement and outreach successes of FTC's Legal Services Collaboration, which created a robust and institutionalized partnership with legal aid, many WH-LAIR agencies with enforcement mandates will work with legal aid to increase their enforcement capacity and amplify outreach efforts. For example, DOJ's Civil Rights Division plans meetings with legal aid providers around the country to build on their existing collaboration and information exchange and further institutionalize these relationships; FCC will perform outreach to legal aid to broaden the use of communication tools for people with disabilities such as Telecommunications Relay Service for deaf, hard of hearing, deaf-blind, or those with a speech disability and other provisions under FCC's iCanConnect program;[64] EEOC and DOL are working to strengthen their respective collaborative partnerships with civil legal aid providers who can inform the agency of relevant issues to enhance their enforcement and outreach activities; and DOL is formalizing their collaborative processes, including having a specific designee in each region.

➢ **Advancing evidence-based research, data collection, and analysis.** Building on the insights gleaned from the Civil Legal Aid Research Workshop hosted by DOJ with the support of NSF, WH-LAIR agencies are developing metrics for evaluating whether and how legal aid improves agency programs. Examples include: VA plans to develop a robust data collection strategy to scale up its efforts to identify and address veterans' unmet legal needs; HHS's Administration for Community Living intends to start capturing information about elder abuse and legal assistance; and LSC is undertaking a new national legal needs survey to update the Justice Gap studies of 2005 and 2009. An increasing number of agencies' program evaluations are considering the impact of legal aid on program effectiveness. For example, DOL will soon complete an evaluation of its Face Forward grant for court-involved youth including the legal aid component, and DOI plans to similarly review the role of legal aid in its programs in tribal communities. In addition, the WH-LAIR Working Group on Access to Justice Indicators and Data Collection will release an overview of its activities soon. Finally, the FY 2017 budget request for DOJ's National Institute for Justice includes $2.7 million for a Civil Legal Aid Research Institute, which would address the need for additional academic research regarding civil legal aid and help supplement the evidence base on the impact of legal aid in communities.

"WH-LAIR's big idea is simple: Together we can create more opportunities to grab the next rung on the ladder out of poverty by partnering with legal aid to meet Federal—and global—objectives.

*~Karen Lash
Executive Director, WH-LAIR*

Conclusion

The President signed the Presidential Memorandum formally establishing the White House Legal Aid Interagency Roundtable on the eve of the United Nation's adoption of the 2030 Agenda for Sustainable Development, and with good reason. The 2030 Agenda recognizes on a global scale what WH-LAIR agencies are already doing, as reflected in this Report. We cannot end poverty without access to justice; we cannot protect the most vulnerable among us without access to justice; and we cannot build transparent and accountable government without access to justice.

This Report documents the power of legal aid to help Federal programs, policies, and initiatives that aim to improve the lives of low-income people and underserved populations. WH-LAIR's 22 agencies recognize that improved collaboration with legal aid will bring us all closer to our shared goal of improving the lives of all Americans.

In this next phase of WH-LAIR's work, member agencies will continue to embrace this powerful tool and look for opportunities to incorporate legal aid into Federal programs that increase meaningful access to justice for all, help millions of people meet their basic needs, and raise the quality of life for all in America.

> *The White House Legal Aid Interagency Roundtable has become indispensable in helping the Federal government establish partnerships with legal aid providers that push Federal programming forward and ensure that essential services reach the communities that need them most.*
>
> *~Cecilia Muñoz*
> *White House Domestic Policy Council Director*
> *WH-LAIR Co-Chair*

Appendix A - Presidential Memorandum

THE WHITE HOUSE

Office of the Press Secretary

For Immediate Release   September 24, 2015

September 24, 2015

MEMORANDUM FOR THE HEADS OF EXECUTIVE DEPARTMENTS AND AGENCIES

SUBJECT: Establishment of the White House Legal Aid Interagency Roundtable

By the authority vested in me as President by the Constitution and the laws of the United States of America, and in order to increase the availability of meaningful access to justice for individuals and families and thereby improve the outcomes of an array of Federal programs, it is hereby ordered as follows:

Section 1. Policy. This Nation was founded in part on the promise of justice for all. Equal access to justice helps individuals and families receive health services, housing, education, and employment; enhances family stability and public safety; and secures the public's faith in the American justice system. Equal access to justice also advances the missions of an array of Federal programs, particularly those designed to lift Americans out of poverty or to keep them securely in the middle class. But gaps in the availability of legal aid -- including legal representation, advice, community education, and self-help and technology tools -- for America's poor and middle class threaten to undermine the promise of justice for all and constitute a crisis worthy of action by the Federal Government.

The majority of Americans who come to court do so without legal aid. They may be left by their economic circumstances to face life-altering events -- such as losing a home or custody of children, or escaping domestic violence or elder abuse -- on their own. More than 50 million Americans qualify for federally funded civil legal aid, but over half of those who seek assistance are turned away from legal aid organizations, which lack the funds and staff to meet the demand.

When people come into contact with or leave the criminal justice system, they are likely to face a range of legal issues. A victim of abuse may need a protective order, or a formerly incarcerated individual may need a driver's license reinstated in order to get a job. Access to legal aid can help put people on a path to self-sufficiency, lead to better outcomes in the civil and criminal justice systems, and enhance the safety and strength of our communities. Increased legal resources in a community can also help courts process cases more effectively and more efficiently, saving time and money.

Federal programs that are designed to help the most vulnerable and underserved among us may more readily achieve their goals if they include legal aid among the range of services they provide.

By encouraging Federal departments and agencies to collaborate, share best practices, and consider the impact of legal services on the success of their programs, the Federal Government can enhance access to justice in our communities.

   Sec. 2. <u>Establishment</u>. There is established the White House Legal Aid Interagency Roundtable (LAIR).

   Sec. 3. <u>Membership</u>. (a) The Attorney General and the Director of the Domestic Policy Council, or their designees, shall serve as the Co-Chairs of LAIR, which shall also include a representative from each of the following executive departments, agencies, and offices:

> (i) the Department of State;
> (ii) the Department of the Treasury;
> (iii) the Department of Justice;
> (iv) the Department of the Interior;
> (v) the Department of Agriculture;
> (vi) the Department of Labor;
> (vii) the Department of Health and Human Services;
> (viii) the Department of Housing and Urban Development;
> (ix) the Department of Education;
> (x) the Department of Veterans Affairs;
> (xi) the Department of Homeland Security;
> (xii) the Equal Employment Opportunity Commission;
> (xiii) the Corporation for National and Community Service;
> (xiv) the Office of Management and Budget;
> (xv) the United States Agency for International Development;
> (xvi) the Administrative Conference of the United States;
> (xvii) the National Science Foundation; and
> (xviii) such other executive departments, agencies, and offices as the Co-Chairs may, from time to time, designate.

   (b) The Co-Chairs shall invite the participation of the Consumer Financial Protection Bureau, Federal Trade Commission, Legal Services Corporation, and Social Security Administration, to the extent consistent with their respective statutory authorities and legal obligations.

Sec. 4. <u>Mission and Function</u>. (a) The LAIR shall work across executive departments, agencies, and offices to:

>   (i) improve coordination among Federal programs that help the vulnerable and underserved, so that those programs are more efficient and produce better outcomes by including, where appropriate, legal services among the range of supportive services provided;
>
>   (ii) increase the availability of meaningful access to justice for individuals and families, regardless of wealth or status;
>
>   (iii) develop policy recommendations that improve access to justice in Federal, State, local, tribal, and international jurisdictions;
>
>   (iv) assist the United States with implementation of Goal 16 of the United Nation's 2030 Agenda for Sustainable Development; and
>
>   (v) advance relevant evidence-based research, data collection, and analysis of civil legal aid and indigent defense, and promulgate best practices to support the activities detailed in section 4(a)(i)-(iv).

(b) The LAIR shall report annually to the President on its success in achieving its mission, consistent with the United Nation's 2030 Agenda for Sustainable Development. The report shall include data from participating members on the deployment of Federal resources that foster LAIR's mission.

Sec. 5. <u>Administration</u>. (a) The LAIR shall hold meetings at least three times a year and engage with Federal, State, local, tribal, and international officials, technical advisors, and nongovernmental organizations, among others, as necessary to carry out its mission.

(b) The Director of the Office for Access to Justice in the Department of Justice, or his or her designee, shall serve as Executive Director of LAIR and shall, as directed by the Co-Chairs, convene regular meetings of LAIR and supervise its work. The Office for Access to Justice staff shall serve as the staff of LAIR.

(c) The Department of Justice shall, to the extent permitted by law and subject to the availability of appropriations, provide administrative services, funds, facilities, staff, equipment, and other support services as may be necessary for LAIR to carry out its mission.

(d) The LAIR members are encouraged to provide support, including by detailing personnel, to LAIR.

(e) Members of LAIR shall serve without any additional compensation for their work.

Sec. 6. <u>General Provisions</u>. (a) This memorandum shall be implemented consistent with applicable law and subject to the availability of appropriations.

(b) Nothing in this memorandum shall be construed to impair or otherwise affect:

    (i) the authority granted by law to an executive department, agency, or the head thereof; or

    (ii) the functions of the Director of the Office of Management and Budget relating to budgetary, administrative, or legislative proposals.

(c) This memorandum is not intended to, and does not, create any right or benefit, substantive or procedural, enforceable at law or in equity by any party against the United States, its departments, agencies, or entities, its officers, employees, or agents, or any other person.

                                BARACK OBAMA

                                # # #

Appendix B – WH-LAIR's Engagement with Civil Society

WH-LAIR has engaged with civil society—non-governmental organizations and institutions—since its start in 2012. Through consultations, workshops, and presentations involving civil society, WH-LAIR has exemplified open and accountable government practices and upheld the U.S. Government's commitment to the Open Government Partnership on access to justice.

Consultations and workshops with civil society have informed the work of WH-LAIR and its agencies. These events include:

- *April 2014 Civil Society Consultation on Access to Justice for the United States' Second Universal Periodic Review and hearing before the UN Committee on the Elimination of Racial Discrimination* organized and hosted by American University's Washington College of Law's Center for Human Rights and Humanitarian Law with participation of dozens of organizations
- *May 2015 WH-LAIR Civil Legal Aid Research Workshop* with participation of 45 non-Federal experts
- *September 2016 Civil Society Consultation on Access to Justice Indicators* and *Data Collection* organized by Columbia University School of Law's Human Rights Institute and Fordham Law School's National Center for Access to Justice and hosted by Open Society Foundations with participation of dozens of organizations

Since 2012, WH-LAIR representatives have presented on their activities at a number of civil society-sponsored conferences, events, and webinars. Such engagement has helped WH-LAIR operate openly and transparently. These events have been sponsored by organizations including:

- Access to Justice State Commissions in California, Connecticut, the District of Columbia, and Mississippi
- American Bar Association
- American University Washington College of Law's Center for Human Rights and Humanitarian Law
- Avocats sans Frontières
- Columbia Law School's Human Rights Institute
- Equal Justice Works
- Fordham Law School's National Center for Access to Justice
- Hague Institute for the Internationalisation of Law – HiiL
- International Legal Foundation
- Management Information Exchange
- National Center for Medical-Legal Partnership
- National Health Law Program
- National Legal Aid and Defender Association (NLADA)
- NLADA's Community Oriented Defender Network
- NLADA's Litigation and Advocacy Directors
- Open Society Foundations
- Open Society Justice Initiative
- New York University's Institute of Judicial Administration and Center on Civil Justice
- New York University's Center on International Cooperation
- Pro Bono Net
- Self-Represented Litigation Network
- Voices for Civil Justice

Appendix C - WH-LAIR Contributors

From its inception in 2012 to the issuance of the Presidential Memorandum in 2015 to now, every aspect of WH-LAIR has been a product of collaboration, both in ideas and resources, and a shared vision by many committed individuals in diverse Federal agencies and offices. This appendix lists current and former Federal employees who have led and supported WH-LAIR.

Administrative Conference of the United States
Reeve Bull, Connie Vogelmann⁺, Matthew Wiener*, Amber Williams
U.S. Agency for International Development
Laura Adams, Jennifer Lewis, Tony Pipa, Keith Schulz, John Simpkins*, Andrew Solomon⁺, Ilyse Stempler, David Young
Consumer Financial Protection Bureau
Richard Cordray*, Mary Griffin, Gail Hillebrand, Wendy Weinberg, Evan White⁺
Corporation for National and Community Service
William Basl, Erin Dahlin⁺, Asim Mishra, Wendy Spencer*
U.S. Department of Agriculture
Yeshimebet Abebe, David Grahn⁺, Melissa McClellan, James Murray, Jennifer Nicholson, Doug O'Brien, Bianca Oden, Frederick Pfaeffle Arana, Jeffrey Prieto*
U.S. Department of Education
Sean Addie, Jay Chen, James Cole*, Phavy Cunningham, Laura Ginns⁺, Susan Inman, Paul Riddle
U.S. Department of Health and Human Services
Lauren Antelo⁺, Jennifer Burnszynski, Katherine Chon, Alexander Coccia, Rashida Dorsey, Dan Duplantier, Robin Ghernter, Nora Gilligan, Vicki Gottlich, Mark Greenberg, Alixandra Hallen, Seiji Hayashi, Melissa Heitt, Charles Homer*⁺, Mechelle Johnson-Webb, Wilfred Johnson II, Jennifer Joseph, Robert Keith, Judith Kozlowski, Becky Kurtz, Barbara Lacina, Gia Lee, Jim Macrae*, Kristina McBoyle, Kim Meinert, Lisette Mestre, Adrienne Noti, Nisha Patel, William Rivera, Sarah Spector, Vicki Turetsky, Jennie Simpson, Ali Sutton, Damon Waters, Michael Wolf
U.S. Department of Homeland Security
Amanda Baran, Stevan Bunnell*, Katherine Condon, Elizabeth Cedillo-Pereira, Fana Desta, Matthew Gordon, Sarah Harrison⁺, Kevin Landy, Gary Lukowski, Stephen McHale, Mary Ellen Martinet, Kelly Ryan
U.S. Department of Housing and Urban Development
Ronald Ashford, Jad Atallah, Keisha Brooks, Adrienne Buenavista, Nicola Hill, Helen Kanovsky*, Adam Norlander, Tonya Robinson, Carolyn Rosenthal, Maya Rupert⁺, Donald Sherman, Howard Sims, Benjamin Winter
U.S. Department of the Interior
Cheryl Andrews-Maltais, Darren Cruzan, Nicole Hanna, Kathryn Isom-Cloud, Miles Janssen, Lawrence Roberts*, Katherine Scotta, Tricia Tingle⁺, Kevin Washburn
U.S. Department of Justice
Julia Alanen, Bethany Backes, Bill Baer, Virginia Baran, Allen Beck, Marlene Beckman, James Cadogan, Cindy Chang, Brent Cohen, Rena Cutlip-Mason, Silas Darden, Ron Davis, Stuart Delery, Nicole Dennis, Shirlethia Franklin, Joye Frost, Maria Fryer, Shannon Gaskins, Kathi Grasso, Javier Guzman, Rosie Hidalgo, Sam Hirsch, Seri Irazola, Jennifer Kaplan, Steven Lang, Robert Listenbee, Beverly Lumpkin, Karol Mason, Andy Mao, Julie McEvoy, Beth McGarry, Maureen McGough, Jeri Mulrow, Nadine Neufville, Denise O'Donnell, Helaine Perlman, Kathrina Peterson⁺, John Picarelli, Theron Pride, Ruby Qazilbash, Bernardo Rodriguez, Laurence Rothenberg, Priya Sarathy Jones, Philippa Scarlett, Amy Solomon, Cornelia Sorensen Sigworth, Natalia Sorgente, Howard Snyder, Suzanne Strong, Christine Stoneman, Corey Stoughton, Tony West, Darla Wolf

U.S. Department of Labor

Justin Allen, Jacqueline Freeman, Deborah Greenfield, Christopher Lu*, Michelle Massie, Natalia Merluzzi, Jamila Minnicks, Richard Morris, Demetra Smith Nightingale, Kerry O'Brien, Ariel Levinson-Waldman+, Gregory Willis

U.S. Department of State

Daniella Ballou-Aares, Camille Eiss, Lena Gerber, Bob Gifford, Shibani Malhotra+, Tom Malinowski*, Michael Overby, Sarita Vanka

U.S. Department of the Treasury

Brendan Bertagnoll, Sarah Bloom Raskin*, Eduardo Bruera+, Rachana Desai, Jane Dokko, Janice Feldman, Valerie Gunter, Melissa Koide, Rourke O'Brien, Louisa Quittman

U.S. Department of Veterans Affairs

Leigh Bradley*, Sean Clark, Peter Dougherty, Anne Dunn, Lara Eilhardt+, Andrea Finlay, Will Gunn, Steven Reiss, William Russo, Christine Timko, Lisa Yee

Equal Employment Opportunity Commission

Charlotte Burrows*, Edmund Chiang, Gladys Collazo, Vicky Gonzalez, Ana Gonzalez-Joy, Evangeline Hawthorne, Davis Kim+, Kelly Trindel

Federal Trade Commission

Kati Daffan, Charles Harwood, Daniel Kaufman, Edith Ramirez*, Monica Vaca+, David Vladeck

Federal Communications Commission

Ruth Milkman, D'wana Terry, Lauren Wilson+

Legal Services Corporation

Becky Fertig Cohen, Ron Flagg, Mark Freedman, Lynn Jennings, Carlos Manjarrez, Cheryl Nolan, Zoe Osterman+, Jim Sandman*

National Science Foundation

Scott Barclay, Jon Gould*, Mark Hurwitz+, Helena Silverstein*, Susan Sterett, Alan Tomkins

Office of Management and Budget

James Boden, Julie Allen Dingley, Scott Nathan*, Jennifer Park, Kyle Riggs+

Social Security Administration

Ben Belton, Stacey Cole, Frank Cristaudo*+, Ben Gurga, Lisa Martin, Jioni Palmer, Kaelia Plunkett, Stacy Rodgers, Leslie Rogall, Jane Ross, Kelly Tribble Spencer

+ Denotes the agency's official designees to WH-LAIR and WH-LAIR agency advisors.
* Denotes agency principals who attended the February 29, 2016 WH-LAIR Principals' meeting co-chaired by Attorney General Loretta Lynch and Domestic Policy Council Director Cecilia Muñoz.

In addition, the following current and former White House staff have led and supported the activities of WH-LAIR: Roy Austin, Caroline Bettinger-Lopez, Myesha Braden, Carmen Facciolo, Lisa Kohn, Natalia Merluzzi, Tonya Robinson, and Kip Wainscott. WH-LAIR is staffed by DOJ's Office for Access to Justice with the following current and former staff: Bob Bullock, Mark Childress, Melanca Clark, Silvia Dominguez-Reese, Lisa Foster, Helam Gebremariam, Maha Jweied, Jenni Katzman, Karen Lash, Deborah Leff, Stephan Matthews, Daniel Olmos, Andrew Stanner, Anne Traum, and Allie Yang-Green.

Endnotes

[1] The Legal Services Corporation is a Federally-funded, independent nonprofit organization and is a member of WH-LAIR. For purposes of this Report LSC is included in references to "Federal agencies" or "WH-LAIR agencies."

[2] According to the American Bar Association, Interest on Lawyers' Trust Accounts (IOLTA) is a method of raising money for charitable purposes, primarily the provision of civil legal services to indigent persons. The establishment of IOLTA in the United States followed changes to federal banking laws passed by Congress in 1980, which allowed some checking accounts to bear interest. IOLTA programs currently operate in 50 states, the District of Columbia, and the U.S. Virgin Islands. For more information, see *Overview*, AM. B. ASS'N, http://www.americanbar.org/groups/interest_lawyers_trust_accounts/overview.html (last visited Oct. 13, 2016).

[3] Martin Frankel, Carroll Seron, Gregg Van Ryzin & Jean Frankel, *The Impact of Legal Counsel on Outcomes for Poor Tenants in New York City's Housing Court: Results of a Randomized Experiment*, 35 LAW & SOC'Y REV. 419 (2001).

[4] Amy Farmer & Jill Tiefenthaler, *Explaining the Recent Decline in Domestic Violence*, 1 CONTEMP. ECON. POL'Y 158 (2003); *see also* Carolyn Copps Hartley & Lynette M. Renner, *The Longer-Term Influence of Civil Legal Services on Battered Women*, NCJRS 249879 (2016), https://www.ncjrs.gov/pdffiles1/nij/grants/249879.pdf.

[5] Jeffrey Selbin & Justin McCrary, *Got Clean Slate? New Study Suggests that Criminal Record Clearing May Increase Earnings*, (Aug. 25, 2014) http://ssrn.com/abstract=2486867.

[6] Daniel Atkins, Shannon Mace Heller, Elena DeBartolo & Megan Sandel, *Medical-Legal Partnerships and Healthy Start: Integrating Civil Legal Aid Services into Public Health Advocacy*, 35 J. LEGAL MED., 195 (2014).

[7] Laura Abel, *Economic Benefits of Legal Aid*, NAT'L CTR FOR ACCESS TO JUST. (2012) https://ncforaj.files.wordpress.com/2012/09/final-economic-benefits-of-legal-aid-9-5-2012.pdf.

[8] *See* U.S. CENSUS BUREAU, 2015 AMERICAN COMMUNITY SURVEY 1-YEAR ESTIMATES: POVERTY STATUS IN THE PAST 12 MONTHS, Table S1701 (2015).

[9] LEGAL SERVS. CORP., DOCUMENTING THE JUSTICE GAP IN AMERICA 7 (2009), http://www.lsc.gov/sites/default/files/LSC/images/justicegap.pdf.

[10] Mark R. Rank & Thomas A. Hirschl, *The Likelihood of Experiencing Relative Poverty over the Life Course*, PLOS ONE J. (July 22, 2015), http://journals.plos.org/plosone/article?id=10.1371/journal.pone.0133513.

[11] According to The Justice Index, a project of the National Center for Access to Justice at the Fordham Law School, more than 80% of litigants appear without lawyers in matters as important as evictions, mortgage foreclosures, child custody and child support proceedings, and debt collection cases in state courts. The Justice Index 2016, http://www.justiceindex.org/ (last visited Oct. 13, 2016). A 2015 report from the National Center on State Courts, The Landscape of Civil Litigation in State Courts, finds that at least one party was self-represented more than 75% of the time in a sample of common state civil cases from urban courts. NAT'L CTR. ON STATE COURTS & STATE JUSTICE INITATIVE, THE LANDSCAPE OF CIVIL LITIGATION IN STATE COURTS (2015) http://www.ncsc.org/~/media/Files/PDF/Research/CivilJusticeReport-2015.ashx.

[12] Rebecca L. Sandefur, *Money Isn't Everything: Understanding Moderate Income Households' Use of Lawyers' Services*, in MIDDLE-INCOME ACCESS TO JUSTICE, 233 (Michael Trebilcock, Anthony Duggan & Lorne Sossin eds., Toronto, University of Toronto Press 2012).

[13] Rebecca L. Sandefur, *The Fulcrum Point of Equal Access to Justice: Legal and Non-Legal Institutions of Remedy*, 42 LOY. LOS ANGELES L. REV. 973 (2009); *see also* Rebecca L. Sandefur, *Access to Civil Justice and Race, Class and Gender Inequality*, 34 ANN. L REV. SOC. 346, 346-49 (2008).

[14] The Presidential Memorandum identified 21 executive departments, agencies, and offices, to participate in WH-LAIR and gave the Co-Chairs authority to designate additional Federal partners. In the summer of 2016, the Federal Communications Commission joined WH-LAIR.

[15] TTA comes in many forms, depending on the type of program and the corresponding need. It can focus on strengthening program implementation and improving service delivery by sharing effective programs and practices, promoting collaboration among grantees and key stakeholders, disseminating the latest research and information on trends and innovative techniques, and improving practices in data collection, evaluation and analysis. TTA may be delivered by the Federal program staff or an external organization under a TTA contract, through various means such as workshops, convenings, individualized consulting, and online resources. TTA can be mandated by statute or designed by agencies to meet specific needs of a state or local community.

[16] The working group members include ACUS, DOI BIA, DOJ EOIR, DOL, EEOC, HHS, HUD, Treasury IRS, NSF, SSA, USDA, and VA.

[17] The draft report for ACUS's project can be found at: https://www.acus.gov/sites/default/files/documents/Self-Represented-Parties-Administrative-Hearings-Draft-Report.pdf. When available, the final report will be uploaded to ACUS's website, and can be found on the project page: https://www.acus.gov/research-projects/self-represented-parties-administrative-hearings.

[18] Additionally, in March 2016, NSF, in partnership with DOJ's ATJ, issued a solicitation, "US Ignite: Networking Research and Application Prototypes Leading to Smart & Connected Communities," which specifically encouraged applications that could demonstrate a networking technology advancement that improves access to justice, and informs a research agenda and/or identifies technology priorities for civil legal aid. For more information, see NATIONAL SCIENCE FOUNDATION, U.S. IGNITE: NETWORKING RESEARCH AND APPLICATION PROTOTYPES LEADING TO SMART & CONNECTED COMMUNITIES (2016) https://www.nsf.gov/pubs/2016/nsf16553/nsf16553.htm (last visited Sept. 27, 2016).

[19] UN's 2030 Agenda for Sustainable Development, ¶ 75 reads: "The Goals and targets will be followed-up and reviewed using a set of global indicators. These will be complemented by indicators at the regional and national levels which will be developed by member states, in addition to the outcomes of work undertaken for the development of the baselines for those targets where national and global baseline data does not yet exist." G.A. Res. 70/1, ¶ 75 Transforming our World: The 2030 Agenda for Sustainable Development (Oct. 21, 2015).

[20] Civil society is the "third sector" of society, along with government and business. It comprises a wide array of non-governmental organizations and institutions including community organizations, non-profit organizations, and academics.

[21] HENRY J. KAISER FAMILY FOUND., KEY FACTS ABOUT THE UNINSURED POPULATION (2015), http://kff.org/uninsured/fact-sheet/key-facts-about-the-uninsured-population/ (last visited Sept. 29, 2016).

[22] For more information about medical-legal partnerships, see NATIONAL CENTER FOR MEDICAL-LEGAL PARTNERSHIP, http://medical-legalpartnership.org (last visited Sept. 27, 2016).

[23] See *Civil Legal Aid Supports Federal Efforts to Help People Access Health Care*, CASE STUDIES, WHITE HOUSE LEGAL AID INTERAGENCY ROUNDTABLE, www.justice.gov/lair/wh-lair-case-studies (last visited Sept. 27, 2016).

[24] U.S. DEP'T OF HOUS. AND URBAN DEV., 2015 ANNUAL HOMELESS ASSESSMENT TO CONGRESS 1 (2015).

[25] *Id.*

[26] See *Civil Legal Aid Supports Federal Efforts to Help People Exit Homelessness and Stay Housed*, CASE STUDIES, WHITE HOUSE LEGAL AID INTERAGENCY ROUNDTABLE, www.justice.gov/lair/wh-lair-case-studies (last visited Sept. 27, 2016).

[27] See U.S. Dep't of Hous. and Urban Dev., State CDBG Guide to National Objectives and Eligible Activities 2-38, https://www.hudexchange.info/onecpd/assets/File/CDBG-State-National-Objectives-Eligible-Activities-Chapter-2.pdf.

[28] In 2015, legal service providers were grantees or sub-grantees in 120 out of the total of 380 SSVF grants, making up 34% of the SSVF's total grants. All SSVF grantees are required to at least provide a link to legal services via referral. In addition, in 2015, the SSVF Program added specific guidance in its Program Handbook on how potential grantees may incorporate legal services into their grant applications.

[29] Pew Charitable Trusts, Collateral Costs: Incarceration's Effect on Economic Mobility 4 (2010), http://www.pewtrusts.org/~/media/legacy/uploadedfiles/pcs_assets/2010/collateralcosts1pdf.pdf.

[30] U.S. Dep't of Educ., 2013-2014 Civil Rights Data Collection: A First Look 3 (2016), http://www2.ed.gov/about/offices/list/ocr/docs/2013-14-first-look.pdf.

[31] *Id.*

[32] See *Civil Legal Aid Supports Federal Efforts to Help Keep Children in School & Civil Legal Aid Supports Federal Efforts to Strengthen Families*, Case Studies, White House Legal Aid Interagency Roundtable, www.justice.gov/lair/wh-lair-case-studies (last visited Sept. 27, 2016).

[33] See *Civil Legal Aid Supports Federal Efforts to Keep Americans Working*, Case Studies, White House Legal Aid Interagency Roundtable, www.justice.gov/lair/wh-lair-case-studies (last visited Sept. 27, 2016).

[34] See Office of Family Assistance, TANF Program Policy Questions and Answers 10, 19, 20, http://www.acf.hhs.gov/ofa/resource/q-a-use-of-funds?page=all (last visited Oct. 13, 2016).

[35] Nat'l Ctr for Injury Prevention and Control, National Intimate Partner and Sexual Violence Survey 2 (2011), http://www.cdc.gov/violenceprevention/pdf/nisvs_executive_summary-a.pdf.

[36] Nat'l Ctr. on Elder Abuse, Statistics/Data https://ncea.acl.gov/whatwedo/research/statistics.html (last visited Sept. 29, 2016).

[37] Int'l Labor Office, Profits and Poverty: The Economics of Forced Labor 11 (2014), http://www.ilo.org/wcmsp5/groups/public/---ed_norm/---declaration/documents/publication/wcms_243391.pdf.

[38] See, e.g., Am. Sociological Ass'n, Race, Ethnicity, and the Criminal Justice System (2007), http://www.asanet.org/sites/default/files/savvy/images/press/docs/pdf/ASARaceCrime.pdf (showing disparities in offending and victimization by race); Brookings Inst., Crime and Incarceration on America's Poor (2016) https://www.brookings.edu/research/u-s-concentrated-poverty-in-the-wake-of-the-great-recession/ (last visited Sept. 29, 2016).

[39] See *Civil Legal Aid Supports Federal Efforts to Help Prevent Elder Abuse; Civil Legal Aid Supports Federal Efforts to Help Prevent Domestic Violence; Civil Legal Aid Supports Federal Efforts to Help Human Trafficking Victims*, Case Studies, White House Legal Aid Interagency Roundtable, www.justice.gov/lair/wh-lair-case-studies (last visited Sept. 27, 2016).

[40] Eligible legal aid includes proceedings for protective/restraining orders or campus administrative protection/stay-away orders; family, custody, contract, housing, and dependency matters, particularly for victims of intimate partner violence, child abuse, sexual assault, elder abuse, and human trafficking; immigration assistance for victims of human trafficking, sexual assault, and domestic violence; intervention with creditors, law enforcement (e.g., to obtain police reports), and other entities on behalf of victims of identity theft and financial fraud; intervention with administrative agencies, schools/colleges, tribal entities, and other circumstances where legal advice or intervention would assist in addressing the consequences of a person's victimization.

[41] Press Release, Fed. Trade Comm'n, FTC Survey for 2011 Shows an Estimated 25.6 Million Americans Fell Victim to Fraud (Apr. 19, 2013), http://www.ftc.gov/opa/2013/04/fraudsurvey.shtm (last visited Sept. 29, 2016)

[42] FED. TRADE COMM'N, FTC RELEASES ANNUAL SUMMARY OF CONSUMER COMPLAINTS (2016), https://www.ftc.gov/news-events/press-releases/2016/03/ftc-releases-annual-summary-consumer-complaints (last visited Sept. 29, 2016).

[43] 13 CONSUMER FIN. PROTECTION BUREAU MONTHLY COMPLAINT REP. 11 (2016), http://s3.amazonaws.com/files.consumerfinance.gov/f/documents/Monthly_Complaint_Report_-_July_2016.pdf.

[44] BUREAU OF JUSTICE STATISTICS, VICTIMS OF IDENTITY THEFT, 2014 (2015), http://www.bjs.gov/content/pub/pdf/vit14_sum.pdf.

[45] Richard Power, *Child Identity Theft: New Evidence Indicates Identity Thieves are Targeting Children for Unused Social Security Numbers*, CARNEGIE MELLON CYLAB (2011), https://www.cylab.cmu.edu/files/pdfs/reports/2011/child-identity-theft.pdf.

[46] See *Civil Legal Aid Supports Federal Efforts to Help Protect Consumers*, CASE STUDIES, WHITE HOUSE LEGAL AID INTERAGENCY ROUNDTABLE, www.justice.gov/lair/wh-lair-case-studies (last visited Sept. 27, 2016).

[47] See WH-LAIR: ENHANCING ENFORCEMENT THROUGH COLLABORATION WITH CIVIL LEGAL AID (2016), https://www.justice.gov/lair/file/875631/download.

[48] U.S. DEP'T OF HOUS. AND URBAN DEV., 2015 ANNUAL HOMELESS ASSESSMENT TO CONGRESS 4 (2015)

[49] See *Civil Legal Aid Supports Federal Efforts to Help Veterans and Servicemembers*, CASE STUDIES, WHITE HOUSE LEGAL AID INTERAGENCY ROUNDTABLE, www.justice.gov/lair/wh-lair-case-studies (last visited Sept. 27, 2016).

[50] For more information about legal clinics in VA facilities, see VETERANS AFFAIRS, FREE LEGAL CLINICS IN VA FACILITIES (2016), http://www.va.gov/ogc/docs/LegalServices.pdf.

[51] VA surveys veterans to identify needs of homeless veterans including their legal needs. Each year, VA's Project CHALENG (Community Homelessness Assessment, Local Education and Networking Groups) surveys local veterans, VA staff and community participants on homeless veterans' needs. The survey includes specific questions about different kinds of legal needs of homeless veterans. The most recent CHALENG report for FY 2015 finds that five of the top ten unmet needs involved legal assistance: eviction/foreclosure prevention, child support issues, outstanding warrants/fines, discharge upgrades, and restoring a driver's license. Several of the other top ten unmet needs also have legal components, including family reconciliation assistance, credit counseling, and government benefits. See U.S. DEP'T OF VETERANS AFFAIRS, COMMUNITY HOMELESSNESS ASSESSMENT, LOCAL EDUCATION AND NETWORKING GROUPS FACT SHEET (2016), http://www.va.gov/HOMELESS/docs/CHALENG-2015-factsheet-FINAL-0616.pdf.

[52] See *Civil Legal Aid Supports Federal Efforts on Behalf of Tribes and Tribal Members*, CASE STUDIES, WHITE HOUSE LEGAL AID INTERAGENCY ROUNDTABLE, www.justice.gov/lair/wh-lair-case-studies (last visited Sept. 27, 2016).

[53] Public Law 83-280 (commonly referred to as "Public Law 280" or "PL-280") altered the usual allocation of criminal jurisdiction in Indian country and authorized the states of Alaska, California, Minnesota, Nebraska, Oregon, and Wisconsin to prosecute most crimes that occurred in Indian country. For more information, see https://www.justice.gov/usao-mn/Public-Law%2083-280.

[54] See *Civil Legal Aid Supports Federal Efforts to Help Americans with Disabilities*, CASE STUDIES, WHITE HOUSE LEGAL AID INTERAGENCY ROUNDTABLE, www.justice.gov/lair/wh-lair-case-studies (last visited Sept. 27, 2016).

[55] For more information about the P&A programs, see Nat'l Disability Rights Network, Protection & Advocacy Systems Programs (2010), http://www.ndrn.org/images/Documents/Media/Press_kit/NDRN_P__A_programs_2010.pdf.

[56] ADMIN. CONFERENCE OF THE U.S., SSA REPRESENTATIVE PAYEE: SURVEY OF STATE GUARDIANSHIP LAWS AND COURT PRACTICES (2015), https://www.acus.gov/sites/default/files/documents/SSA%2520Rep%2520Payee_State%2520Laws%2520and%2520Court%2520Practices_FINAL.pdf.

[57] Todd D. Minton & Zhen Zheng, Jail Inmates at Midyear 2014, Bulletin. (Washington, DC: Bureau of Justice Statistics, 2015), NCJ 248629.

[58] Amy L. Solomon, *In Search of a Job: Criminal Records as Barriers to Employment*, 270 NAT'L INST. OF JUST. J. 42 (2012), http://www.nij.gov/journals/270/Pages/criminal-records.aspx (last visited Sept. 29, 2016).

[59] See *Civil Legal Aid Supports Federal Efforts to Help People with Criminal Records Make a Successful Reentry* CASE STUDIES, WH-LAIR, www.justice.gov/lair/wh-lair-case-studies (last visited Sept. 27, 2016).

[60] U.S. DEP'T OF JUSTICE, EXEC. OFFICE FOR IMMIGRATION REVIEW, FY 2015 STATISTICS YEARBOOK F1, https://www.justice.gov/eoir/page/file/fysb15/download. This figure includes those cases completed "in absentia."

[61] INGRID EAGLY & STEVEN SHAFER, AMERICAN IMMIGRATION COUNCIL, ACCESS TO COUNSEL IN IMMIGRATION COURT 18-21 (Sept. 2016), https://www.americanimmigrationcouncil.org/sites/default/files/research/access_to_counsel_in_immigration_court.pdf. Additionally, according to a study conducted in the New York immigration courts, individuals with lawyers are five times more likely to prevail in their cases than those without a lawyer. NEW YORK IMMIGRATION REPRESENTATION STUDY, ACCESSING JUSTICE II: A MODEL FOR PROVIDING COUNSEL TO NEW YORK IMMIGRANTS IN REMOVAL PROCEEDINGS 1 (2012), http://www.cardozolawreview.com/content/denovo/NYIRS_ReportII.pdf.

[62] In this Report, the phrase "unaccompanied child" or "unaccompanied immigrant child" carries the same meaning as "unaccompanied alien child (UAC)," which is defined as follows: UAC is one who has no lawful immigration status in the United States; has not attained 18 years of age, and with respect to whom; 1) there is no parent or legal guardian in the United States; or 2) no parent of legal guardian in the United States is available to provide care and physical custody. See *About Unaccompanied Children's Services*, U.S. DEPT. OF HEALTH & HUMAN SERVS., http://www.acf.hhs.gov/orr/programs/ucs/about (last visited Sept. 27, 2016).

[63] For more information on LEP resources including state courts-related LEP resources, see https://www.lep.gov/resources/resources.html.

[64] Under iCanConnect, officially known as The National Deaf-Blind Equipment Distribution Program, individuals who are deaf-blind and meet certain income guidelines can receive free equipment designed to make telecommunications, Internet access, and advanced communications services more accessible. For more information about iCanConnect, see https://www.fcc.gov/general/national-deaf-blind-equipment-distribution-program.